GREAT CHRISTIAN THINKERS

Kierkegaard

PETER VARDY

Dr Peter Vardy is lecturer in the Philosophy
of Religion at Heythrop College, University
of London. He is a former Chair of the
Theology Faculty Board of the University
of London, where he runs undergraduate
and postgraduate courses on Kierkegaard.
Among his previous books are *The Puzzle
of God, The Puzzle of Evil, The Puzzle of Ethics* and *The Puzzle of the Gospels.*

Praise for Other Titles in the Great Christian Thinkers Series

AUGUSTINE Richard Price
'... admirably clear, concise, and though sometimes critical, written with great sympathy and understanding of Augustine's problems, and of the historical context within which he was labouring.' MICHAEL WALSH, *BUTLER'S LIVES OF THE SAINTS* AND *BOOK OF SAINTS*

FRANCIS & BONAVENTURE Paul Rout
'This book meets a real need ... a painless way into Bonaventure's life and thinking, both as a philosopher, a man of prayer and as a great Franciscan.' SISTER FRANCES TERESA, OSC, THE COMMUNITY OF THE POOR CLARES, ARUNDEL

JOHN OF THE CROSS Wilfrid McGreal
'We are greatly indebted to Fr Wilfrid McGreal for bringing alive in such an accessible way the mysticism and mystery of St John of the Cross.' GEORGE CAREY, ARCHBISHOP OF CANTERBURY

THOMAS MORE Anne Murphy
'This superb piece of scholarship sheds new light on the enduring importance of the unity between Thomas More's life and thought. Anne Murphy shows how this large-hearted Christian was a great European and an outstanding example of personal and public integrity.' GERALD O'COLLINS, GREGORIAN UNIVERSITY, ROME

KIERKEGAARD Peter Vardy
'This is a fascinating introduction to Kierkegaard's prophetic insights into the nature of Christian faith, insights which we desperately need to ponder today.' GERALD HUGHES, AUTHOR OF *GOD OF SURPRISES*

SIMONE WEIL Stephen Plant
'Stephen Plant portrays the immense strength and the touching vulnerability of Simone Weil, the complex nature of her convictions, and the startling and continuing relevance of her views today.' DONALD ENGLISH, CHAIRMAN OF THE WORLD METHODIST COUNCIL

GREAT CHRISTIAN THINKERS

KIERKEGAARD

Peter Vardy

SERIES EDITOR: PETER VARDY

Triumph
Liguori, Missouri

Published by Triumph
An Imprint of Liguori Publications
Liguori, Missouri

Library of Congress Cataloging-in-Publication Data

Vardy, Peter.
    Kierkegaard / Peter Vardy. — 1st U.S. ed.
        p.   cm. (Great Christian thinkers)
    Includes bibliographical references and index.
    ISBN 0-7648-0115-5
    1. Kierkegaard, Søren, 1813–1855. I. Title. II. Series.
BX4827.K5V37   1997
230'.044'092—dc21
[B]   96-52495

Originally published in English by HarperCollinsPublishers Ltd under the title: *Kierkegaard* by Peter Vardy.

First U.S. Edition 1997
01 00 99 98 97   5 4 3 2 1
Printed in the United States of America

This book is dedicated to you, the reader.

Contents

Abbreviations

AC	*Attack upon Christendom*, tr. Walter Lowrie
CA	*The Concept of Anxiety*, tr. Reidar Thompte
CUP	*Concluding Unscientific Postscript*, tr. Walter Lowrie and David Swenson
ED	*Eighteen Edifying Discourses*, tr. Walter Lowrie (OUP)
EO	*Either/Or*, tr. David and Lillian Swenson
FSE	*For Self Examination*, tr. Walter Lowrie
FT	*Fear and Trembling*, tr. Alastair Hannay (Penguin)
J	*Journals*, ed. and tr. Howard and Edna Hong
PF	*Philosophical Fragments*, tr. David Swenson
PH	*Purity of Heart is to will one thing*, tr. Douglas Steere (Harper Torchbooks)
SD	*Sickness unto Death*, tr. Walter Lowrie
SLW	*Stages on Life's Way*, tr. Howard and Edna Hong
TC	*Training in Christianity*, tr. Walter Lowrie
WL	*Works of Love*, tr. Howard and Edna Hong

Except where indicated, all the above are published by Princeton University Press.

Introduction

This is a book about a remarkable man – yet in an important sense it is not about this man at all. Søren Kierkegaard died in Copenhagen, Denmark, at the age of forty-two in 1855. His writings had little influence in his lifetime and after his death, even with the translation of some of his works into German, he was barely known. Today, although now internationally accepted as one of the world's great thinkers, few people have more than a scant idea about his writings.

This is not essentially an academic book. Hopefully, however, it is academically sound if by this is meant that it is faithful to Kierkegaard's thought and to his intention. The intended audience is the same as his own – namely you, the single individual who reads these words. The intended purposes are also very similar to his own, namely:

1. To help you, the reader, to think through the meaning and purpose of your life and what Christianity means today. This may seem obvious and to be something that every person knows, but Kierkegaard did not think this was the case.
2. To reintroduce Christianity into a world which has largely forgotten what the word means.
3. To show the limitation of reason and of modern philosophy.

In addition, there is a fourth and important purpose – to show the essential unity of Kierkegaard's thought and to encourage you to read his works for yourself. There can be no substitute for this and these words are but a pale reflection of his own – although hopefully they may sometimes be more accessible in an impatient age.

Finally, there is an important by-product – to provide a riposte on behalf of traditional Christianity to the modern theologians and philosophers who have transformed eternal truth into a human construct. Kierkegaard is a man for our time since he can provide a reply to the rational voices of our age when most other voices are muted.

This book, and Kierkegaard's works, show little that is new. Kierkegaard did not wish to found a new philosophic school, he did not see himself as an innovator. He was the Fire Chief who, when a fire breaks out, takes charge of proceedings. The matter is urgent, time is short and action is required – the Fire Chief may forcefully point out what needs doing, but, in the matter of your own life, the response is down to you – and it is to you that this book is dedicated.

Kierkegaard's Life

Søren Kierkegaard's father, Michael Pedersen Kierkegaard, was born in a poor village in Jutland where he suffered from cold, hunger and loneliness. One day, at the age of eleven, Michael Pedersen was on the wild Jutland heath caring for cattle. He was alone, cold and wet and, because of his sufferings, he stood on a little hill, raised his hands to heaven and cursed God who was so cruel as to allow him to suffer so much. The memory of this curse was to remain with him for the rest of his life. His uncle rescued him by taking him to Copenhagen to work in his clothing business. He eventually inherited his uncle's fortune, built up a successful cloth and trading business and became a wealthy man. He married at thirty-eight and retired from business at the age of forty. His wife died two years after the marriage and, before the accepted mourning period was complete, on 26 April 1797, he married again – to Ane Sørendatter Lund, who had been a servant in the house before his wife's death. The first child was born on 7 September 1797 – four months after the marriage. Søren was the last of seven children from the second marriage.

Søren Aabye Kierkegaard was born on 5 May 1813 in Copenhagen, Denmark's small capital city. He died there on 11 November 1855. A brother and sister died before he was nine years old and his two remaining sisters as well as one of his brothers died before he was twenty-one. Kierkegaard's father had a great influence on him as a child – although there is no reference in his writings to his mother, who did not appear to be at all important in the family. Kierkegaard's father was a melancholy man who developed, after his retirement, a passion for philosophy. He would have friends in to dinner and they would discuss philosophy (mainly German) into the night. Kierkegaard used to sit and listen to the conversation and to be fascinated by the swings in the argument. It was his father who helped develop Kierkegaard's imagination, taking him by the hand and walking him up and down inside the house talking to him and conjuring up in his imagination the streets of the great cities of Europe, the father pointing out all the sights, sounds and smells to the young boy.

At school, Kierkegaard was always the odd one out, partly because he was physically weak, and partly due to his dress. His father made him wear shoes rather than boots like the other children as well as skirts to his coat. He was nicknamed 'Choirboy', because his clothes resembled those of children in the charity schools, and also 'Søren Sock' because of his father's previous occupation. He had a devastating wit and used this instead of physical strength to protect himself from the jibes of his fellows. The Dean of Vibourg, who was at school with Kierkegaard, told a story which illustrates his personality:

Professor Mathiessen, the teacher in German, was an exceedingly weak man who never had any authority over us. Once when the horseplay in class had gone very far – it was quite wild in all his classes – when the pupils had made a complete meal with butter-bread, sandwiches and beer, and had toasted one another with formal prosits, Professor Mathiessen was about to go out and report the affair to the Headmaster. The rest of us surrounded Mathiessen with prayers and fair promises, but Søren said only, 'Please tell the Headmaster that this is always what goes on in your class' – whereupon Mathiessen sat down and made no report. (QUOTED IN WALTER LOWRIE, *A SHORT LIFE OF KIERKEGAARD*)

Kierkegaard's religious upbringing was rigorous and old-fashioned. As he describes it in *Point of View on my Life as an Author*:

> *As a child I was strictly and austerely brought up in Christianity; humanly speaking, crazily brought up. A child crazily travestied as a melancholy old man. Terrible! What wonder then that there were times when Christianity appeared to me the most inhuman cruelty...*

Kierkegaard entered the Royal Guards for his military service but was discharged after three days as medically unfit. At the age of seventeen, in 1830, he entered Copenhagen University. He worked hard, particularly in the first year, enjoying the exploration of ideas and he read widely. He seemed happy, thoroughly enjoying university life, loving the theatre and the pleasure of conversation and being at the centre of many parties: he appeared to be making a determined effort to break loose from his rigorous upbringing. He was popular – although people were nervous of him, his wit could be cruel. He was one of the intellectual and cultural luminaries of Copenhagen society and was known to everyone. At the age of twenty, in 1833, he began his *Journals*, which represent one of the most extraordinary such undertakings ever published and which give marvellous insights into his thought. His wide ranging University reading contrasted with the conventional but highly orthodox religiousness of his home. His attention to his studies waned and he ran up considerable bills – which his father had to settle – as he lived the life of a wealthy young 'man about town'. His apparent carefree life, however, contrasted with feelings of deep depression. On one occasion he returned from a party where he had been full of wit and gaiety and his journal records that he felt like shooting himself.

Then, in his twenty-second year, what Kierkegaard referred to as 'the great earthquake' occurred. This may refer to one of two things – either to his discovery of his father's childhood curse or else to his discovery that his father had seduced his mother while she was a servant in his house and soon after, or even before, the death of his father's first wife. Both would have had a considerable effect on Kierkegaard as he considered his father to be the model religious man. It was this event that Kierkegaard saw as marking the transition from youth to adulthood and it also marked a 'distance' between him and his father which was not bridged until shortly before his father's death on 8 August 1838. Kierkegaard had a profound religious experience some months before his father died. He dated his report of this experience precisely – 19 May, 10.30 a.m.:

> There is such a thing as an indescribable joy which glows through us unaccountably as the Apostle's outburst is unexpected: 'Rejoice, and again I say Rejoice!' – Not a joy over this or that, but full jubilation, 'with hearts and souls and voices': 'I rejoice over my joy, of, in, by, at, on, through, with my joy' – a heavenly refrain, which cuts short, as it were, our ordinary song; a joy which cools and refreshes like a breeze, a gust of the trade wind which blows through the Grove of Mamre to the eternal mansions.

The reference to the 'Grove of Mamre' is a reference to Genesis 18:1: 'The Lord appeared to him by the oaks of Mamre, as he sat in the tent door in the heat of the day.' Kierkegaard does not, however, dwell on this experience a great deal – it happened and it was part of his journey towards being a Christian but, looking back at the end of his life, he thought that throughout the whole of his life he was being educated into what it was to be a Christian.

Following the death of his father at the age of eighty-one, Kierkegaard became a wealthy man and inherited a substantial house in Copenhagen. He was working for his theological examinations and passed these in July 1840. In 1837, before his father's death, he had met a very young girl, Regina Olsen, and had fallen in love with her, but she was only fourteen and too young to be wooed and he had to work at his studies. She was confirmed in

1840 at the age of sixteen and this was the recognized step which meant that he could approach her. He was deeply in love and possibly also saw that Regina provided the hope for him of a normal life. He proposed to her and was accepted. However, he began to suffer from a tremendous melancholy and increasingly felt that he could not go through with the marriage. We cannot know the precise reasons but it was at least partly due to his unhappy childhood, the secrets of his dead father, his own personality and the task in life he felt he had to undertake – he loved her too much to submit her to a marriage which he thought would make her unhappy. Finally, after much agonizing, he sent back the engagement ring with this brief letter:

In order not to put more often to the test a thing which after all must be done, and which being done will supply the needed strength – let it then be done. Above all, forget him who writes this, forgive a man who, though he may be capable of something, is not capable of making a girl happy.

To send a silken cord is, in the East, capital punishment for the receiver; to send a ring is here capital punishment for him who sends it.

Regina was desolated and begged him to have her back – he could not explain why he would not, because he loved her too much. He believed that only by showing himself to be a scoundrel could she turn away from him and be free to love someone else. Otherwise she would have clung to him and would not have been free to find happiness elsewhere. Kierkegaard was convinced Regina could not find happiness with him and because his love was so great he could not want anything else. He continued to love her for the rest of his life – so much so that one glance from her sent him to Berlin for five months. She later became engaged to a former teacher and she and Kierkegaard had no real communication thereafter. When Kierkegaard died, he left her everything he had.

Kierkegaard defended his master's thesis, 'On the Concept of Irony', in September 1841. In November, he left for the first of four visits he was to make to Berlin – on this first occasion he attended Schelling's lectures. For the rest of his life Kierkegaard lived alone, with a servant, and had no close friends and dedicated himself to his writing. He loved walking the streets of Copenhagen and talking to people and also much enjoyed the company of his young relatives, to whom he was a figure of fun and whose visits were keenly anticipated. He was a well-known figure in the city and in the years from 1841 onwards lived an apparently carefree life – often being seen at the theatre. It was, however, something of a double life. He would sometimes go to the theatre at the interval just to be seen and when the next act started would slip back to his rooms to continue his writing far into the night.

Between 1842 and 1845 he produced some of his most important pseudonymous works – *Either/Or*, *Repetition* and *Fear and Trembling* (1843), *Philosophical Fragments* and *The Concept of Anxiety* (1844) and *Concluding Unscientific Postscript* and *Stages on Life's Way* (1845), although at the same time he was also writing some of his greatest *Edifying Discourses* – sermons designed to be read aloud. In December 1845 he was involved with a public and very bitter dispute with the *Corsair* – a rather scandalous newspaper which defied the strict censorship of its time and relied heavily on gossip about the wealthier classes – which he decided to attack and which in turn attacked him. The upshot of this was that in early 1846 he was made into a figure of fun in Copenhagen, with the *Corsair* producing caricatures of him and making fun of his bandy legs so that he could no longer walk the streets without being mocked.

Kierkegaard continued his writing, but with a change in style and approach, and his books became more obviously religious. In 1847 he published *Works of Love* and *Edifying Discourses*, in 1848 *Christian Discourses* and in 1849 *The Lilies of the Field and the Birds of the Air* and *Three Discourses on Communion on Fridays* as well as, under the pseudonym Anti-Climacus, *Sickness unto Death* – which harks back to issues he had dealt with in earlier works. This was followed, in 1850, by *Training in Christianity*. In 1849 he also wrote *Point of View on my Life as an Author*, although this was not published until after his death. This book attempted to explain his authorship and what he was trying to do. Throughout this period he was a regular and committed churchgoer and wrote numerous sermons – he even considered taking a post as a pastor.

From 1849 onwards he became increasingly disillusioned with the established Danish Church which he considered was unfaithful to Christian discipleship. He lived in increasingly difficult financial circumstances as he had been living all his life on his father's money and had earned little from his books. In 1854–5, shortly before his death, he directly attacked the Danish Church and its ministers in a series of bitter articles including some published in his own broadsheet, the *Instant*. These articles have been collected together in a book entitled *Attack upon Christendom*. He also ceased going to church and on his deathbed refused to receive communion from a minister who he considered to be a state employee rather than a servant of Christ – he would have liked to have taken communion from a lay person but that was not possible. He died in November 1855, giving thanks to God, looking forward to eternity and completely at peace.

(This brief sketch of Kierkegaard's life is due to many sources but in particular to Walter Lowrie's *A Short Life of Kierkegaard*, which, although somewhat dated and now out of print, is still the best resource. The Princeton editions of *Philosophical Fragments* and *Concluding Unscientific Postscript* also have relevant details.)

Kierkegaard's lonely childhood; his melancholy and religious father who was highly intelligent yet deeply affected by his curse of God on the Jutland heath; his father's love for his first wife and his seduction of a housekeeper and his preoccupation with philosophy; Kierkegaard's active imagination, his unhappy childhood and the way he was made to stand out from his fellows and to

---

hone and develop his wit and irony to protect himself; his dissolute life in Copenhagen once he left home; his rapprochement with his father and his religious experience; his engagement to and love of Regina and the stifling of his love for her; his few friends and his cruel treatment at the hands of the Copenhagen crowd following the *Corsair* affair; his unusual appearance and his loneliness can all be invoked to explain his writings in psychological terms or they can be seen in a positive way – because freedom from external distractions such as friends, security and family laid him open to discovering what it means to live in a relationship with God.

Kierkegaard himself would have considered the details of his life as irrelevant, and to concentrate on Kierkegaard rather than his message is to miss the point. It is, therefore, with his message and his thought – and not with his motivations or his psychological state – that the remainder of this book is concerned.

2

Socrates and Jesus

Socrates and Jesus were both remarkable men who were unjustly condemned to death, who faced their death relatively calmly, who believed in a life after death and who have had a tremendous impact on later generations. Kierkegaard set out to compare and contrast these two individuals in *Philosophical Fragments*, which was published under the pseudonym Johannes Climacus in 1844. Kierkegaard wrote many of his books under pseudonyms so that he could adopt a perspective slightly different from his own.

Although the story of Jesus is well known, that of Socrates is less so. Socrates was proclaimed by the Delphic Oracle to be the wisest man in Athens. When this was reported to him he could not understand it as he felt that he knew nothing. Socrates, therefore, set out to prove the oracle wrong. He did this by questioning people – by questioning all those who thought themselves wise about the source of their wisdom. In the course of this questioning, it rapidly became clear to Socrates that those who thought themselves wise were, in fact, not so. Their answers were confident enough to begin with, but under Socrates' close examination it was apparent that they had few grounds for their claim to wisdom. Socrates thus came to the conclusion that what the oracle was really saying was that that person was wisest who knew that he knew nothing.

During this questioning, Socrates acquired a young and delighted following who much enjoyed seeing their revered elders being shown to be a good deal less wise than they first appeared.

This of course made Socrates highly unpopular and in due course he was brought to trial on the charge of corrupting the young and teaching against the gods. The method of trial involved five hundred of the free citizens of Athens being allowed to vote on the guilt or innocence of the accused individual. Socrates' friends tried to persuade him to hire skilled orators, trained in the best techniques of persuasion. These orators prided themselves on being able to sway the crowd, and this was decisive for an acquittal. Socrates, however, totally rejected this approach because it had nothing to do with the search for truth and, as he had previously shown, the orators as a group had no basis at all to their claims to wisdom and learning.

We have a record of the trial written by Socrates' friend and pupil Plato – although how much of this is historically accurate and how much is Plato putting his own thought onto Socrates' lips we cannot know. We do know, however, that Socrates, as recorded in the book, presented a reasoned and well-argued defence which seems to be irrefutable intellectually, but the crowd are persuaded by the prosecuting orators to vote for conviction which carried the death penalty. It was open to Socrates to propose some lesser punishment such as banishment or a substantial fine, and Socrates' friends tried to persuade him to do this as it was likely that such a plea would have been accepted. Socrates, however, refused saying that any such proposal would represent a confession of guilt, and as he was not guilty he could not agree. The sentence of death was thus confirmed and Socrates was required to take hemlock. An interval elapsed, however, before he was required to take the drug and Plato records Socrates' conversations with his friends. Socrates is given the chance of escaping from the city but he refuses to do this, claiming that he has lived all his life under the laws of Athens and would not reject them now. According to these laws he has been condemned to death and he will therefore accept the sentence. The book ends with Socrates taking the hemlock while his friends mourn: Socrates is calm throughout and engages in quiet philosophic speculation with his friends about what happens after death.

The parallels with Jesus are obvious – although given the account of Jesus in Gethsemane, Jesus may have faced death less calmly than Socrates. Are, then, Socrates and Jesus to be considered as broadly similar? It is with this question that Kierkegaard is concerned. In some ways *Philosophical Fragments* is a work of christology as it addresses the question of who Jesus was. Is Jesus to be considered as a remarkable man, able to provide real insights into the human condition and how life should be lived, or is he something more? And, if so, what difference does this make?

Eternal Truth

Socrates, Climacus considers, is a human teacher. Once we learn something, it really does not matter who taught us. Socrates is part of the whole vast human enterprise which, over the centuries, gradually develops greater and greater knowledge about the universe and how it works. With each generation the frontiers of our knowledge are extended. A few individuals may be decisive in breaking through barriers of understanding at particular points, but the human race as a whole is contributing to the development of human understanding about the way the world works.

Johannes Climacus' task, in *Philosophical Fragments*, is to examine the position if Jesus Christ *is* radically different from Socrates or any similar man or woman. In the case of a philosopher or other thinker, the moment at which someone comes to understand truth and the individual through whom this understanding is reached are largely irrelevant. If Jesus is essentially different to Socrates then it will be Jesus' life that is his message. Jesus is claimed to be God and can, therefore, reveal eternal truths. He is not just teacher but also saviour, because he confronts people and can show them that they are in error. Jesus himself will thus be of decisive importance for the individual who encounters him and the moment when such an individual comes to learn the eternal truth that Jesus Christ has to teach will also be decisive. The error that Jesus reveals is not just a matter of objective knowledge – he reveals something about the person's inmost self, about what it is to be a human being.

If he was just bringing people to see truths that he or she could have worked out for themselves given the necessary ability and insights, then Jesus would not be essentially different from Socrates. If he is different, then the truth that Jesus brings must be of a different order:

> *The truth then is that the learner owes the Teacher everything. But this is what makes it so difficult to effect an understanding; that the learner becomes as nothing and yet is not destroyed; that he comes to owe everything to the Teacher and yet retains his confidence; that he understands the Truth and yet that the Truth makes him free; that he apprehends the guilt of his error, and yet that his confidence rises victorious in the Truth.* (PF 38)

If Jesus Christ is the teacher, then the individual who comes to know the truth through him must be the learner. If Jesus Christ is decisively different from Socrates, then the eternal truth which he brings can be truth of a radically different kind to Socratic truth which would not otherwise be available to us. Eternal truths are not truths we can come to learn on our own account – human beings therefore need help to gain access to these truths, they have to be revealed. What is more, they are a different type of truth to normal, objective knowledge – eternal truth has to do with what it is to be a self, what it is to be a human being.

The Effects of Sin

Kierkegaard considered that Jesus Christ, the God-Man, did not simply provide eternal truth by living and dying on a 'once and for all' basis – God also teaches today, in our own time, through the Bible and can thus speak directly to the individual. Kierkegaard came from an Augustinian and Lutheran background and he considered the effects of sin on human beings to be profound. Modern philosophers in the Reformed tradition such as Alvin Plantinga and Cornelius Van Tyl talk of 'the noetic effects of sin' – in other words, the effect that sin has had on human abilities to know eternal truths. What this approach does not take into account is a point that Kierkegaard emphasizes – the truth that Jesus reveals is not a matter of doctrines or propositional knowledge, it is truth about human beings and their relationship to God. Reformed Epistemologists tend to overlook this – yet in one way theirs is a helpful manner of expressing Climacus' point – human sin has deprived people of the condition necessary for them to accept eternal truth and only God can restore this condition and also communicate this truth. Anyone who does not accept the truth is in error – and this error is due to sin. What is not so clear is whether Climacus is referring to *individual* sin or to the Fall – whereby the whole of humanity has been affected by *original* sin. Both approaches give rise to difficulties. On one reading of the text, Climacus appears to be referring to individual sin:

> *In so far as the learner was in Error, and now receives the Truth and with it the condition for understanding it, a change takes place within him like the change from non-being to being. But this transition from non-being to being is the transition we call birth. But now one who exists cannot be born; nevertheless, the disciple is born. Let us call this transition the New Birth ... the disciple who is born anew owes nothing to any man, but everything to his divine Teacher.* (PF 23–4)

On this view, the individual appears to have the condition to understand eternal truth at birth but loses it by his or her own action during his or her life. On this interpretation, questions can be asked about when this loss takes place. There seems to be no reason why it is necessary for all human beings to sin and therefore to lose the condition and, indeed, one might then expect some children in their innocence to be radically different from corrupt adults. The individual, on this model, would lose the condition and then have it restored again and the time-frame of this process seems problematic in the extreme.

It may be, therefore, that Climacus is talking of the effects of original sin, which has blighted the ability of all human beings to see the truth. Due to original sin, human beings lost their original capacity or condition for accepting the centrality of the human relationship to God. On this basis, Christ's coming would have been crucial as it would restore the condition to all human beings and also be a way of communicating eternal truth.

There is an alternative possibility which would also be consistent with original sin being decisive in the loss of the condition. This is to hold that original sin has given human beings the false impression that they are able to apply reason successfully to the mystery of God. It is, perhaps, not a coincidence that Adam and Eve's problems started when they ate from the tree of knowledge. Karl Barth held a view not dissimilar to this, and although I do not maintain that Climacus held this view, it would be consistent with his argument.

Climacus considers human beings and God to be separated by a great gulf due to error and sin, and this chasm has to be bridged. What is more, the chasm is infinitely wide – after all, God is God, the creator of the universe, and human beings are very pale creatures in comparison. Only God can bridge this enormous gap: human beings are impotent to do so. The incarnation achieved the bridging of the chasm whereby God chose to become a man. Climacus considers what motive could move God to bridge the gap

— what could move God since God is God and cannot be moved by anything outside himself?

> Moved by love, the God is then eternally resolved to reveal himself. But as love is the motive, so love must also be the end; for it would be a contradiction for the God to have a motive and an end which did not correspond. His love is a love of the learner, and his aim is to win him. For it is only in love that the unequal can be made equal, and it is only in equality or unity that an understanding can be effected ...

This idea of God being motivated by love, and indeed, essentially being love, is one that is endorsed by the Franciscan approach to theology and set out by Bonaventure (cf. Paul Rout's *Francis and Bonaventure* in the Great Christian Thinkers series). To illustrate his point, Climacus tells the parable of a king 'who loved a maiden of lowly station in life'. The king faces an immediate problem if his love is genuine: how can he bridge the great gulf between himself and the girl so that genuine love can be possible? The king does not seek blindly obedient service, he seeks love, and if love is to occur the girl must be free to reject or to love him for himself. There are two possible ways the great gulf between the king and the girl can be bridged:

> The king might have shown himself to the humble maiden in all the pomp of his power, shedding a glory over the scene, and making her forget herself in worshipful admiration. Alas, and this might have satisfied the maiden, but it could not satisfy the king, who desired not his own glorification but hers. It was this that made his grief so hard to bear, his grief that she could not understand him ... (PF 36)

The girl would be overwhelmed by the king's majesty: she would be awed, terrified and obedient, but love would be impossible. This way of bridging the gulf is not, therefore, an option. However there is an alternative. The king could go to the girl in the appearance of 'the lowliest of persons. But the lowliest of all is one who must serve others.' The king, therefore, out of love must go to the girl in the form of a servant and must hope that the girl will love him for himself – and not for his power and glory. Of course he runs a risk: he risks the girl not loving him. However, only if the king makes himself equal with the girl does love become possible.

The analogy is obvious and Climacus spells it out clearly. God comes to earth as a man, out of love. Jesus Christ is thus essentially different from Socrates, Gandhi or any other great religious leader since only he is God, only he can be the teacher of eternal truth. The incarnation is decisive as it bridges the gulf between humanity and God. This story is also helpful in showing the type of truth that God wishes to communicate. The king does not want the girl to learn objective facts about himself, he wishes her to fall in love with him. On this understanding, God does not wish human beings to learn theological doctrines but to enter into a genuine relationship with God.

The Absolute Paradox

The idea that Jesus, an ordinary looking man walking around Palestine nearly two thousand years ago, could also be God, the creator and sustainer of the universe, is not a reasonable one. God is the unknown, the absolutely unlike. As Kierkegaard says:

There is an infinite, radical, qualitative difference between God and man. (J 697)

Humans make the mistake of conceiving God in anthropomorphic terms. God, Kierkegaard maintains, is qualitatively different from human beings – God is not the highest superlative of the human. To show the dangers of failing to take the unknowability of God seriously, Kierkegaard says:

The fundamental derangement at the root of modern times ... consists in this: that the deep qualitative chasm in the difference between God and man has been obliterated. (J 6075)

The Jesuit theologian Karl Rahner referred to God as Holy Mystery – indeed Rahner's guiding motif was the nearness of God as mystery, and Kierkegaard's emphasis on God as the unknown is not alien to this. If God is the unknown, the absolutely unlike, how can God become man? How can the infinite and the finite meet? How can the eternal and the temporal, the creator and creature become one? Rationally and logically this must be rejected. Jesus may indeed be considered to have been a wonderful man, a great ethical teacher, a religious inspiration – but he cannot rationally be held to be God, or so Climacus maintains. Climacus considers that the traditional Christian claim about the incarnation, that Jesus Christ was both fully God and fully human, cannot be rationally understood or accepted. It is a paradox – in fact, the Absolute Paradox, as it is the bringing together of two things which are most unlike – God and man:

The supreme paradox of all thought is the attempt to discover something that thought cannot think. (PF 46)

There are two possible reactions to the Absolute Paradox: the first is offence and the second is faith. Confronted by the Absolute Paradox, reason will collide with it, will wrestle with it, will consider it – and reject it. Reason (philosophy) will take offence at the paradox and stand aside from it and Kierkegaard considers that it is entirely *reasonable* that it should do so. Writing under the pseudonym Anti-Climacus, to be distinguished from Johannes Climacus (the pseudonym of *Philosophical Fragments* and the *Concluding Unscientific Postscript*), but in this respect showing great similarity, he says:

Offence has essentially to do with the composite term God and man, or with the God-Man ... The God-Man is the paradox, absolutely the paradox, hence it is quite clear that the understanding must come to a standstill before it. (TC 83;86)

Whereas the Johannes Climacus pseudonym is used to denote a philosophical analysis of Christianity by someone who does not himself profess to have faith, Anti-Climacus, by contrast, stands for the position of someone who is writing from a faith perspective.

Today, most philosophers of religion in Britain and America operate firmly within a Kantian framework – religion must be within the limits of reason alone. If this is so, the traditional claim of the incarnation must be rejected. Rationally – according to reason – the claim that Jesus is both fully God and fully man is *not* logical and if reason reigns supreme it should be rejected. The rational individual will, therefore, reject the Absolute Paradox because it is a paradox, because it offends against reason, 'because it is absurd' (PF 52). If reason is the highest then there is nothing more to say – reason can only reject that which goes against reason.

Climacus expresses the point succinctly:

When the Reason takes pity on the Paradox, and wishes to help it to an explanation, the Paradox does not indeed acquiesce, but nevertheless finds it quite natural that the Reason should do this; for why do we have our philosophers if not to make supernatural things trivial and commonplace? (PF 66)

Faith and the Individual Will

It might appear from what has been said so far that faith is a question of individual will. The individual must decide for him- or herself whether to set reason aside and to accept the paradox. However, Climacus considers this is only part of the picture – faith is crucially a gift, given by 'the Teacher'. However, Kierkegaard does not accept the seemingly logical consequence that some are given faith whilst others are not. He rejects predestination and determinism and believes passionately in the freedom of each individual. Faith is a gift, but it is a gift that has to be received and striven for as well. It is as if the two poles meet, just as two persons meet in a relationship. Precisely how the polarities come together, however, Kierkegaard does not explicitly specify. The approach to faith as a gift and yet as something that has to be striven for is one adopted by many major theologians including Aquinas, Luther and Barth. Kierkegaard's position, therefore, is faithful to the mainstream Christian tradition, although the tension between the two elements is not more easily resolved because of this.

Although Kierkegaard was by no means the first to make the claim that faith went beyond reason, Kierkegaard's great genius was to work out the consequences of this. Part of his tremendous contemporary relevance lies in his argument that reason is not the highest. Rational philosophy does not reign supreme – there is something higher, and that is faith. Tertullian asked: 'What has Athens to do with Jerusalem?' and St Paul wrote: 'We preach Christ crucified, to the Jews a stumbling block and to the Greeks foolishness'. If offence is the response of reason to the Absolute Paradox, then there is another response as well – faith. Faith involves the commitment of an individual's life in a subjective relationship with God. When faith is absent, all that the individual sees when considering the figure of Jesus is an extraordinary man. Kierkegaard maintains that, if the Christian story is true, there is much more to the figure of Jesus than this.

Kierkegaard is a profoundly religious author and he uses his philosophic skills to try to bring individuals to see for themselves what Christianity requires – but this is essentially a matter for each individual. Climacus puts it well:

If anyone proposes to believe, i.e. imagines himself to believe, because many good and upright people living here on the hill have believed, i.e. have said that they believed ... then he is a fool. (PF 129)

Whether the individual responds or not is a matter that he or she must decide, but the individual, Kierkegaard considered, should respond on his or her own account and not because of the influence of a third party or a social group. A person today may be brought up in a Christian culture or may hear the Christian message, but this in itself will not be enough to engender faith – faith is something that must be accepted or rejected individually. Faith, like love, is essentially something that involves each individual: a person ought not to fall in love because another says it is a good idea, and nor should a person have faith on these grounds.

A contemporary of Jesus and someone living today ('the disciple at second hand', in Kierkegaard's phrase) are in exactly the same position. Both have access to certain information about Jesus – the one by observation, and the other by reading the New Testament and by hearing about the Jesus story from others. It is true that the contemporary may have more factual information than the person who is alive today, but more factual information is not going to make the difference between faith and offence, between acceptance and rejection of the Absolute Paradox. Judas, the Pharisees and many others had first-hand knowledge of Jesus, but they did not accept he was God – this is an individual step of faith. It is a response or commitment to the Teacher, an acceptance of truth, a new birth. Clearly these are all identifiable Christian categories but they are categories that dominate *Philosophical Fragments* and which form a crucial part of the mosaic which Kierkegaard's thought represents.

To sum up, Kierkegaard considers that any merely human teacher (like Socrates) is in an essentially different position from Jesus. Jesus, as God, reveals truths that would not otherwise be accessible. The claim that Jesus is both God and man is, however, not *reasonable* – it will elicit either offence or faith.

Having raised the issue of faith and the related issue of truth, we must now consider how Kierkegaard deals with these issues.

3

Truth as Subjectivity

Kierkegaard wrote *Philosophical Fragments*, which discussed the possible difference between Socrates and Jesus outlined in the previous chapter, in 1844. He regarded this as a much more difficult book to write than the *Concluding Unscientific Postscript* which was completed just over a year later, although the latter is generally regarded as his principal work of philosophy. Like *Philosophical Fragments*, it was written under the pseudonym Johannes Climacus. At the end, Kierkegaard makes Climacus' standpoint clear:

> *The undersigned, Johannes Climacus, who has written this book, does not give himself out to be a Christian; he is completely taken up with the thought how difficult it must be to be a Christian* ... (CUP 545)

Climacus sets out a critique of traditional ways of understanding truth, all of which are objective. The objective approach to knowledge relies on reason and, as we saw in the previous chapter, Kierkegaard considered that reason and faith are opposed. What is more, the objective approach makes the individual irrelevant as nothing is staked on objective facts – they need not affect an individual's life. Faith, by contrast, has to do with a relationship and relationships are essentially subjective.

The claim that Jesus was God and man is the Absolute Paradox which cannot be understood by reason and cannot be established by historical enquiry. What is more, the most that any historical enquiry could establish is an approximation of the truth and there would never be enough certainty for the life-changing transformation that faith involves. Faith, for Kierkegaard, requires an inward transformation affecting one's very self and this is radically different from a simple acceptance of factual propositions. Faith requires a transformation of the individual so that the whole of his or her life is lived in a new way, and this the factual or objective approach to knowledge of religious claims avoids.

Belief that God exists or even belief that Jesus was God is not the same as Christian faith. Kierkegaard quotes the Letter of James: 'You believe in God? You do well. The devils also believe – and tremble'. In other words, the devils believe *that* God exists, they do not 'believe in' or centre their lives on God. I may believe *that* the world is round because I have been told this is the case and have seen photographs, but Christopher Columbus believed *in* the world being round and staked his life on it when he attempted to sail round a world which others considered to be flat.

Various questions in life can be looked at either objectively or subjectively – for instance what it means to get married, what it means to die or what it means to pray. Objectively, the first of these might involve consideration of the marriage service, the formalities involved, the legal implications and the like, whilst the second might deal with questions about whether a human person survives death, whether the soul alone survives or whether there is a new body, whether one retains one's memories and so on. However, such objective questions leave out the passionate interest of the individual in these issues and Kierkegaard considered that the really important issues were raised when these questions were addressed subjectively. For instance, what does it mean for me and the way I live my life that I shall survive death? What effect will this have on all my actions and how will my life be transformed? These are questions of a different order to objective questions. Columbus's whole life was affected by his belief that the world was round and Kierkegaard's point is that faith should have a similar, subjective impact.

People who are considered to be wise may accumulate much objective knowledge, but this knowledge is not religiously or existentially significant. Kierkegaard puts it this way:

> ... what is most difficult of all for the wise man to understand is precisely the simple. The plain man understands the simple directly, but when the wise man sets himself to understand it, it becomes infinitely difficult ... the more the wise man thinks about the simple ... the more difficult it becomes for him. (CUP 143)

Kierkegaard's complaint is against philosophers, theologians and others who busy themselves building up more and more learning and lose touch with the simple. In particular, they lose touch with the essential nature of faith and fail to address the really important issues such as what it means to have faith and how this affects them as single individuals. A person can become so stuffed with theological or philosophical knowledge that he or she never gets round to *living* the simple life of faith. Human beings busy themselves with worldly, temporal tasks and so lose interest in the real issue of how to live. Questions such as 'How should I live?' or 'What does it mean for me to have faith?' can mistakenly seem, with much learning, to become irrelevant. Kierkegaard thinks that most philosophers are good talkers and writers but fail to express anything significant with their lives. As he says:

> The police thoroughly frisk suspicious persons. If the mobs of speakers, teachers, professors, etc., were to be thoroughly frisked in the same way, it would no doubt become a complicated criminal affair. To give them a thorough frisking – yes, to strip them of the clothing, the changes of clothing ... to frisk them by ordering them to be silent, saying: Shut up, and let us see what your life expresses, for once let this be the speaker who says what you are. (J 2334)

Instead of living in a world of words that have ceased to have any impact, philosophers, theologians and teachers should be judged by how they live. An individual's life is the best expression of what he or she believes – not the words that are said. Indeed Kierkegaard wishes to bring people to be silent, to cease to take refuge in language and instead to consider who they are before God.

Theologians may reflect deeply and read many books. They may acquire much knowledge, but this does not make them Christians. Kierkegaard puts it like this (my emphasis):

When the question of truth is raised in an objective manner, reflection is directed objectively to the truth, as an object to which the knower is related. Reflection is not focused upon the relationship, however, but upon the question of whether it is the truth to which the knower is related ... Let us take as an example the knowledge of God. Objectively, reflection is directed to the problem of whether this object is the true God; subjectively, reflection is directed to the question whether the individual is related to something **in such a manner that his relationship is in truth a God-relationship.** (CUP 178)

Kierkegaard and Hegel

At the time Kierkegaard was writing, the dominant philosophical system in Denmark was that of the German philosopher Hegel (1770–1831). Hegel considered that Christianity was to a certain extent true, his dialectical method saw truth emerging in human history and philosophy was essentially superior to theology. God, or Absolute Spirit, was, for Hegel, not a being or spirit who created and sustains the universe – instead 'God' as the Absolute Idea attained self-consciousness through the rationality of the human mind. Essentially, Hegel reinterpreted the traditional idea of revelation and of Jesus' incarnation. Hegel still revered Christianity but saw it as no more than an expression of his philosophy of history. Truth was emerging through the development of reason. Christianity was to a certain extent true, and it could be regarded as partly true and partly false that Jesus was God.

This position Kierkegaard totally rejected. Instead of Hegel's stress on a dialectical approach to knowledge which effectively means embracing opposing positions and bringing them together (portrayed by Kierkegaard as a position involving 'Both/And') and Hegel's stress on the dominance of reason and philosophy, Kierkegaard substituted the disjunction 'Either/Or' (either Jesus was God or he was not) and the primacy of faith over reason. Hegel explained away the paradox of the God-Man by saying it was to a certain degree true; Kierkegaard considered that the paradox had to be confronted and either accepted or rejected:

There has been said much that is strange, much that is deplorable, much that is revolting about love, but the most stupid thing ever said about it is, that it is to a certain degree ... Let [a person] consider Christianity. Let him be offended, he is still human; let him despair of ever himself being a Christian, he is yet perhaps nearer than he believes; let him fight to the last drop of blood for the extermination of Christianity, he is still human – but if he is able to say: it is true to a certain degree, then he is stupid. (CUP 205)

Hegel's philosophy made human individuals essentially irrelevant whereas for Kierkegaard each and every individual was of supreme and paramount importance. This disjunction between Hegel and Kierkegaard is still present in Christianity today, with Hegelian thought having given new philosophic impetus to an understanding of Christianity which emphasizes the primacy of the community or 'people of God'. This was also an Old Testament idea, although for the Hebrew prophets God was always central and criticized the community of Israel and individuals within it. Kierkegaard provides a contrast to the community-based approach by emphasizing the primacy of the individual and the individual's life of faith which is lived out in community.

Kierkegaard recognized that the objective approach to truth has advantages:

> ... *the objective way deems itself to have a security which the subjective way does not have (and, of course, existence and existing cannot be thought in combination with objective security); it thinks to escape a danger which threatens the subjective way and this danger is at its maximum: madness. In a merely subjective determination of the truth, madness and truth become in the last analysis indistinguishable, since they may both have inwardness ... Don Quixote is the prototype for a subjective madness in which the passion of inwardness embraces a particular, finite fixed idea ...* (CUP 173–5)

Kierkegaard's point is that if truth is just determined by what someone is personally passionate about (i.e. a 'merely subjective determination of the truth') then there is no way of distinguishing someone who is effectively mad or deluded (like Don Quixote) from someone who has faith. Many commentators on Kierkegaard have taken the phrase 'truth is subjectivity' to mean that if an individual wholly and passionately embraces and lives by a particular idea, then this idea will be true for him or her. They assume that Kierkegaard is dismissing the whole idea of objective truth and making the final determinant of truth a particular individual's subjective state. This type of approach was to give birth to a whole movement in philosophy called Existentialism which, essentially, demanded that individuals should 'be authentic to themselves' and avoid bad faith or inauthenticity. It was this authenticity, some philosophers considered, that determined the truth. This, however, is a travesty of Kierkegaard's position.

As can be seen from the above quote, Kierkegaard clearly recognized that just being passionately subjective about a particular claim to truth was not enough to make something true. People are passionate about a whole raft of ideas – fascism, communism, racism, nationalism – but this does not make these ideas true. Kierkegaard says that anyone who simply embraces a 'particular, finite, fixed idea' is in danger of madness, and he uses Don Quixote to illustrate this. Passion, subjectivity and inwardness alone do *not* make something true.

The God-Relationship

Kierkegaard's argument is essentially directed towards God and the incarnation of Jesus Christ. We have seen that Kierkegaard considered that *either* Jesus was God *or* he was not – but it cannot be proved to be true. However, lack of proof does not mean that this central Christian claim is not true. Either it is or it is not. The key issue is that for an individual to simply assent to the objective truth of the incarnation (by, for instance, saying the creed or simply agreeing that the statement is true) does not mean that the person has faith. The objective truth of the incarnation (if, indeed, it is true) has to be believed in the face of the apparent absurdity of the paradox and 'lived out' in a life of faith, it has to be appropriated by the individual so that it affects the whole of his or her life. Until this happens, the truth does not become true for the individual, it remains 'at a distance'.

This point is well illustrated by C. S. Lewis in his Narnia story, *The Voyage of the 'Dawn Treader'*. He tells how Aslan, the Lion, comes to Lucy when she calls him:

> 'Oh Aslan,' said she, 'it was kind of you to come.'
>
> 'I have been here all the time,' said he, 'but you have just made me visible.'
>
> 'Aslan!' said Lucy almost a little reproachfully. 'Don't make fun of me. As if anything I could do would make you visible!'
>
> After a little pause he spoke again.
>
> 'It did,' said Aslan. 'Do you think I wouldn't obey my own rules?'

Lucy's calling Aslan did not make it true that he was there – Aslan was not some creation of her imagination. However, until she called him and he appeared it was not true *for her* that he was present. Kierkegaard's point is that the nature of Christian truth is such that unless we relate ourselves to it subjectively, we cannot 'know' it. One cannot be 'told', one has to come to 'see' for oneself.

Kierkegaard asks where there is more truth – in the objective or the subjective way. The objective way of seeking truth aims to minimize risk, it is based on reason, proof and justification. The subjective way, however, is fraught with risk: because there is no objective certainty, because there is no proof that a subjective commitment is correct, there is a much greater degree of vulnerability. However, it is only in subjectivity that the individual becomes engaged with the truth as a human being, objectively he or she can stand removed from it and contemplate it neutrally, as a bystander:

> Now when the problem is to reckon up on which side there is more truth, whether on the side of one who seeks the true God objectively and pursues the approximate truth of the God-idea; or on the side of one who, driven by the infinite passion of his need of God, feels an infinite concern for his own relationship to God in truth ... the answer cannot be in doubt. If one who lives in the midst of Christendom goes up to the house of God, the house of the true God, with the true conception of God in his knowledge and prays, but prays in a false spirit; and one who lives in an idolatrous community prays with the entire passion of the infinite although his eyes rest upon the image of an idol; where is there most truth? The one prays in truth to God though he worships an idol; the other prays falsely to the true God, and hence worships in fact an idol. (CUP 179–80)

Kierkegaard's claim is *not* that by worshipping an idol passionately, belief in the idol becomes true. What he is claiming is that when dealing with God the crucial point is the manner of one's relationship with God. In other words, *are you or are you not in a God-relationship?* If you are in a God-relationship, then what you are related to is God whatever name you may give to it. Similarly the other way round, if you are *not* in a God-relationship, then whatever the name you give to whatever you say you are related to, you are not in fact related to it. For Kierkegaard, religion has to do with the individual living out a relationship with God. This is probably the cornerstone around which all Kierkegaard's writings are built. '*Essentially*,' Kierkegaard says, '*it is the God-relationship that makes a man a man*' (CUP 219).

If faith is to do with a relationship with God, then faith must necessarily be subjective. In many ways there are parallels with love – you do not determine whether you are in love by being able to talk about your beloved, by being able to describe him or her and explain his or her background and aptitudes. Instead it is your relationship that is decisive – are you in a love relationship? The same applies to God. The question for faith is, effectively, 'Is God at the centre of your life? Are you in a love-relationship to God?'. You cannot answer this question by reciting theological doctrines or by pointing to the books you have read or the objective truths you say you believe. The answer is to be found only by looking inside yourself and seeing whether God is, indeed, at the centre of your life and whether the whole of your life is determined by and focused on the relationship with God.

Objective Uncertainty

Kierkegaard's definition of truth *and* of faith is:

> *An objective uncertainty held fast in an appropriation-process of the most passionate inwardness is the truth ... without risk there is no faith ... If I am capable of grasping God objectively I do not believe, but precisely because I cannot do this I must believe.* (CUP 182)

The reference to 'objective uncertainty' is to the fact that God's existence cannot be proved nor can Jesus' status as God be justified – both are matters for belief. Faith means staking one's life on something, with total passion, knowing that there is no proof and it is always possible one could be wrong. Faith necessarily involves risk – Kierkegaard describes it as being 'suspended over 70,000 fathoms' (CUP 183). The individual relies on faith alone and that places him or her in a very vulnerable position without the safety and security that are supposed to come with rational proofs.

Faith is not adherence to a set of doctrinal propositions. Faith involves inwardness, it involves living out a relationship with God. A person cannot live out a subjective relationship merely by being part of a crowd or a group, each person has to live the relationship as an individual. The idea of being a Christian as a matter of course is a contradiction in terms – you cannot fall in love as a matter of course or be in love merely because you are a member of a society that talks about love.

Kierkegaard is rigorous in his approach; either Christianity is true or it is false. What it cannot be is a little bit true. If it is true then it demands that everything else be placed in second place to living out the relationship with God. If it is not, then it is irrelevant. Kierkegaard wishes his reader to face the challenge 'either all – or nothing'. If Christianity is true it demands nothing less than the whole of a person's life.

Pilate's question 'What is truth?' (cf. CUP 206) is a detached, objective question. If he had asked the subjective question 'What, in truth, have I to do?' he would never have condemned Jesus. This latter question would have been a matter for Pilate's subjectivity and he could not have washed his hands of this sort of question.

The idea that 'truth is subjectivity' has considerable contemporary relevance in discussion of ecumenical questions. Inter-faith dialogue as well as dialogue between different Christian Churches tends to concentrate on doctrines, rituals and similar objective matters. If Kierkegaard's approach to subjectivity is taken, then a very different position emerges – the issue then becomes whether individuals in different faith communities are or are not genuinely 'living in the truth' or living in a relationship to the absolute which Christians call God. A Muslim may call this absolute Allah and Hindus may see this absolute as having many different interpretations. However, the Muslim, Hindu and Christian who are passionately trying to 'live the relationship' may have much more in common and be much closer to God than different Christians who may assent to the same objective truth claims but who do not share the God-relationship.

If it is possible that Christianity is true, if it is possible that one day there will be a judgement, then the judgement will not be on what doctrines have been accepted but on how each individual has subjectively 'taken on board' and lived out his or her faith. 'As you have lived, so have you believed,' claimed Kierkegaard. It is not a person's words but an individual's life which is the best picture of faith.

To illustrate this, Kierkegaard tells the story of visiting a Copenhagen churchyard and sitting on a bench. Then, as today, there was a high hedge surrounding his seat and he suddenly heard a voice of an old man very close to him who was talking to a child of about ten. He learnt that the little boy was the old man's grandson and they were standing by a freshly dug grave – that of the old man's son and the boy's father. It quickly became clear that the old man's son had abandoned his faith in the interest of pursuing philosophy and had then died. The old man's faith was his strength and hope, yet his son had thought there was something higher than faith and he had thereby sought and lost what was most important of all and the father had been unable to communicate with him. Kierkegaard said:

The venerable old man with his faith seemed to be an individual with an absolutely justified grievance, a man whom existence had mistreated because a modern speculation, like a change in the currency, had made property values in the realm of faith insecure. (CUP 216)

Faith is the highest that any individual can attain, yet modern speculative philosophy mocks faith and makes it out to be nothing. This Kierkegaard refused to accept. If faith is the highest, then reason has no right to cheat people out of faith – it is not possible to go further than faith. Faith is the highest and most difficult demand. It is not something that one can achieve and then move on, it has to be lived out hour by hour, day by day, month by month and year by year for the whole of one's life. It is totally demanding, challenging, uncomfortable and lonely.

We have seen that, for Kierkegaard, truth is subjectivity in that subjective truth involves an individual living out a relationship with God and that there is no objective proof of the validity of this relationship. Faith therefore involves risk. However, if Kierkegaard is not to succumb to the charge of relativism, it is necessary that he provide some criteria for what it means to live in a relationship with God and how an individual can know he or she is in such a relationship. This is dealt with in Chapter 8 – prior to this it is necessary to look at Kierkegaard's stages of life.

4

The Aesthetic Stage

Kierkegaard analyses three 'stages' in life and the relationship between these three is of central importance in understanding his whole authorship. In several books he uses love as the focus for looking at the relationship between the stages, and this analysis also throws light on his views on the relationship between men and women.

Kierkegaard is a master of irony (his doctoral thesis was on the Socratic concept of irony) and of indirect communication. His message is seldom obvious. Although he writes with great depth and subtlety about the aesthetic and ethical stage, it is important to understand that his primary purpose is to encourage people to see their barrenness and emptiness. He analyses them through the pen of pseudonyms. The three stages will be outlined in this and the next two chapters.

The person in the aesthetic stage rejects the ethical norms and the values of society and is instead dedicated to constructing his or her own identity either through living in the world of ideas and the intellect or through the pursuit of pleasure, albeit pleasure of a sophisticated kind. The aesthetic life can be devoted to any temporal goal – power; money; reputation; hobbies – indeed anything which preoccupies people in the temporal world. Pleasures found in this way have to be repeated again and again in order to continue the enjoyment. Kierkegaard uses seduction as an example of the way love is used by the aesthete, but this is no more than a good example of the aesthetic life.

'In Vino Veritas'

Plato's *Symposium* is a discussion on love and Kierkegaard has a similar dialogue called 'In Vino Veritas', which appears in his book *Stages on Life's Way*. It is set in a banquet where a number of people state their views on women (I am grateful to Gregor Malantschuk's excellent book *Kierkegaard's Way to the Truth* here). Plato takes his discussion on love in the direction of the higher, spiritual understanding of love, whereas Kierkegaard moves in the opposite direction – towards the denial of the eternal and immersion in the temporal. There are five characters in Kierkegaard's dialogue who speak in turn. Three of these Kierkegaard has used as pseudonyms in previous works:

- The Young Man
- Constantin Constantinus (author of *Repetition*)
- Victor Eremita (author of *Either/Or*)
- The Fashion Designer
- Johannes the Seducer (author of 'Diary of a Seducer' in *Either/Or*)

The Young Man sees the erotic relationship between men and women as amusing. People devote their whole life to love of another, their individuality is taken over yet no one can define what love is:

> *Who would not feel alarmed if time and again people suddenly dropped dead around him or has a convulsion without anyone being able to explain the reason for it? But this is the way erotic love intervenes in life ... since erotic love expresses itself in loving a one and only, a one and only in the whole world.* (SLW 36)

Love is meant to be spiritual, yet it is motivated and consummated by physical desire which is largely selfish. The two want to come together to form one self, yet this is an illusion. Worse than this, the erotic leads to marriage which is the supreme example of 'society' taking over the individual:

> ... *at the very same moment the species triumphs over the individuals, the species is victorious while individuals are subordinated to being in its service.* (SLW 43)

The Young Man sees contradictions everywhere in the married state. People drift into marriage and the responsibility this imposes. Their individuality is denied and they are obliged to conform to society's values. This leads him to reject any positive relationship to a woman.

Constantin Constantinus is the host of the banquet and he speaks second. He considers women to be merely made for relationships:

> *It is the man's function to be absolute, to act absolutely, to express the absolute; the woman consists in the relational.* (SLW 48)

Constantin is amused at the power women exert over men: '[Men] regard her as an absolute magnitude, and make ourselves into a relative magnitude' (SLW 51). Women are creatures of whim and of pleasure – looked at ethically they do not have an identity of their own but seek their identity in relation to others. They seek to 'lose themselves' in a husband or in children.

Victor Eremita considers that women should never be taken seriously. Any man who takes a woman seriously becomes tied in to foolishness and unpredictability. However, women do have advantages. They can evoke genius, heroism, poetry and sanctity – provided that the man does not attain the woman he desires. If he does, then he is lost. Marriage, Victor maintains, is devoid of meaning and drags an individual down: it leads inevitably to mediocrity. 'A positive relationship with a woman makes man finite on the largest possible scale' (SLW 62). The best way for a woman to awaken her husband to an ideal would be to die or to be unfaithful to him.

The Fashion Designer considers that the whole of a woman's life revolves round fashion:

> *If one wishes to know women, one hour in my boutique is worth more than days and years on the outside.* (SLW 66)

His primary motivation is to make women so ridiculous that they are in chains which corrupt her much more effectively than if she was simply seduced (SLW 70). The Fashion Designer's aim is to prostitute women by making them slaves to fashion. 'So,' he says, 'do not go looking for a love affair, stay clear of erotic love as you would the most dangerous neighbourhood, for your beloved, too, might eventually wear a ring in her nose' (SLW 71).

Johannes the Seducer proclaims that his life is devoted to pleasure:

> *Anyone who, when he is twenty years old, does not understand that there is a categorical imperative – Enjoy – is a fool ...* (SLW 72)

As one might expect, he argues that woman's only function is to satisfy man's desire. Woman is the greatest enticement in the world and most men succumb and become bound by a woman in marriage. He, the Seducer, is one of the small band of 'happy lovers' who have their pleasure without permitting women to tie them down – 'they always nibble at the bait but are never caught' (SLW 84). Johannes speaks in praise of women, in fact he considers them to be 'more perfect' than the male: 'nothing more wonderful, nothing more delicious, nothing more seductive can be devised than a woman' (SLW 76). Women want to be seduced and the devotee of erotic love wants to respond to this by loving as much as possible. No woman is like another:

For what else is woman but a dream, and yet the highest reality. This is how the devotee of erotic love sees her and in the moment of seduction leads her and is led by her outside time, where as an illusion she belongs. With a husband she becomes temporal, and he through her.
(SLW 80)

Diary of a Seducer

In the 'Diary of a Seducer' (in *Either/Or*), Johannes sets out the Seducer's position as well as his technique. His aim is to maximize his pleasure in the pursuit of a young girl, Cordelia. The pursuit is worked through in great detail – here there is no rush to bed but a carefully planned and executed entrapment which the Seducer intends will bring him maximum enjoyment on the journey. The seduction is prolonged as much as possible and when, eventually, he makes love to Cordelia (having first persuaded her to agree to become engaged to him and then breaking the engagement) he loses all interest; the 'fun' of the chase is now over and he wants nothing more to do with her. His sole concern has been his pleasure and, he might say, to teach her that she should pursue a similar aim and not seek to 'lose herself' in him or in others.

Kierkegaard's pseudonym in *Stages on Life's Way* portrays three modern female characters, Marie Beaumarchais, Donna Elvira and Margrethe as representing a typical feminine desire to be 'won' by a man who will remain faithful and contrasts this to Don Giovanni, who has the opposite ambition:

To seduce all girls is the masculine expression of the feminine yearning to let herself be seduced once and for all with heart and soul.

It is easy to see from the above why Kierkegaard can be portrayed as having a contempt for women, but this is to radically misunderstand him. He is writing under pseudonyms and giving the perspectives of different aesthetes who have immersed themselves entirely in the temporal in a search for pleasure which they recognize is transitory. Despair is the inevitable outcome of this position and, coupled with this, other human beings will be regarded in what Kierkegaard considers to be a totally false light. Far, therefore, from praising any of the above positions, Kierkegaard is actually trying to show their bankruptcy. Having said this, he would feel that many women *do* fall into the categories set out above. Like it or not, there are women whose only desire is to marry and to be 'won' by the one true love for the whole of her life just as there are men who see women just as objects of pleasure. However, this is radically different from saying that *all* women or men fall into these categories, still less that they should do so.

Some commentators say that Kierkegaard's pseudonyms do not represent his own views — this is certainly partly true — he uses his pseudonyms to take alternative perspectives other than his own. However, echoes of the pseudonyms' thought can be found in Kierkegaard's private journals. Certainly the pseudonyms put forward a distinctive point of view, but from that point of view Kierkegaard would endorse what is being said.

> ... *what is said by The Seducer (in 'In Vino Veritas') about woman being bait is very true. And strange as it may seem, it is nevertheless a fact that the very thing which makes the seducer so demonic and makes it hard for any poet to contrive such a character is that in the form of knowledge he has at his disposal the whole Christian ascetic view of woman — except that he employs it in his own way. He has knowledge in common with the ascetic, the hermit, but they take off from this knowledge in a completely different direction.* (J 4999)

The aesthete as well as the hermit are similar in that they recognize that their identity is to be found in the inner world rather than through convention — they both see the threat that marriage as an institution represents — however their reactions are very different.

Despair

The aesthete feels in the grip of fate which is beyond his or her control and, above all, is subject to despair. The 'happy' and the 'unhappy' aesthete alike end in despair. The happy aesthete (such as Johannes or Don Giovanni, who represent unreflective masculinity and 'success' in pleasure terms) despair because constant immediate doses of pleasure can never satisfy; they are always transitory, always pointing forward to something else which also does not satisfy. The unhappy aesthete, by contrast, feels the immediate absence of pleasure and also despairs.

The aesthete may come to recognize that whatever he or she does will end in disillusionment – although this may not happen. Many aesthetes continue to live their lives without facing the realization that they are in hidden despair. Experience teaches the aesthete to avoid all human commitment as he considers that commitment will always disappoint and is transitory. However, this lack of commitment results in emptiness and boredom which a person may try to relieve by increased 'doses' of pleasure, which simply make the position worse. Drug abuse might be a good example, but there can be many others. In 'The Rotation Method' in *Either/Or*, Kierkegaard sets out the prudent aesthete's position which is dedicated to avoiding entanglements:

Watch out for friendship ... Never go in for marriage. Married people promise to love each other for eternity. This is easy enough to do but it doesn't mean much, for when one is through with the temporal he will certainly be through with the Eternal as well. If, instead of promising eternal love, the parties concerned might say – until Easter, or until the first of May – this would make sense, for in this case both would actually say something and something which they might possibly stick to. (EO 243)

In the aesthetic stage, a human being sees him or herself as locked into the temporal and there is no way that this can end in anything else but despair. For the aesthete, love involves seeking to be loved – not loving. Gillian Rose maintains that Kierkegaard's book *Repetition* sets out the transition from being loved to being able to love. She puts it like this:

> *Repetition would be the passage from beloved, lovableness, to love-ableness: from knowing oneself loved, 'loveable', to finding oneself graced with a plenitude of being-able-to-love, and thus to risk loving again and again, regardless of any particular outcome, disastrous or successful. To be love-able, to love singularly, to forgive, or release, and hence to love again and again, is the one thing the work can hardly speak.* (GILLIAN ROSE, *THE BROKEN MIDDLE*, BLACKWELL, 23)

As we shall see in a later chapter, non-preferential love, a giving love which seeks nothing in return, is for Kierkegaard the highest form of love – but it is not found in the aesthetic stage.

The Demonic

Judge William, whom Kierkegaard's pseudonym in *Either/Or* portrays as the paradigm of the ethical stage, also throws light on the aesthetic. He analyses the different types of aesthetic existence, all of which he rejects. The judge suggests that at the first level the aesthete's motto might be 'live according to your desires' (EO 155), and the Roman Emperors Caligula and Nero are cited as examples of such an approach. At the second level, the motto might be 'enjoy yourself', which Kierkegaard considers might be represented by living as an epicure. Next comes the aesthetic view which seeks detachment – effectively a stoical independence. In one way or another, these three forms of the aesthetic stage all see enjoyment as the main aim of life.

Beyond this, however, is the person who has seen the bankruptcy of all forms of enjoyment but who refuses to relinquish the aesthetic stage – such an individual sinks into and will not let go of his own despair. It is this stage of the aesthetic which Kierkegaard describes as demonic. Human beings, he says,

> ... are not willing to think earnestly about the Eternal. They are anxious about it, and anxiety discovers a hundred ways of escape. But this, precisely, is what it is to be demonic. (CA 157)

Such an individual is aware of the eternal as a possibility and is repulsed by it: the eternal is specifically rejected. The demonic is shown in closing itself off from and being repulsed by the God who represents the supreme good. It represents 'inclosing reserve', the wish of an individual to turn in on him or herself and to reject God. The individual finds identity in opposing him or herself to the divine. Kierkegaard explains the demonic in terms of Christ's contact with demons in the New Testament: the demonic is anxious about the good, convinced that Christ has come to destroy him, and implores him to 'go away'. Someone suffering the demonic form of anxiety defines themselves against the object which they dread, namely God or the eternal. There is, then, a relation to the divine, but a relation of repulsion. In the parable 'Agnes and the Merman' in *Fear and Trembling* there is a reference to the Merman entering into an absolute relation to the demonic which represents complete rejection of the eternal, thus:

> The demonic has that same property as the divine, that the individual can enter into an absolute relationship to it. (FT 123)

The demonic stands at the opposite pole to the divine and is, like a magnet when facing an opposing pole, repulsed by it. A person in the demonic state is 'closed in' on her or himself because this individual cannot bear to have her or his identity challenged by the divine. By living in the demonic, the individual stands outside the ethical – in a similar way, as we shall see in a later chapter, to the person in the religious stage:

By means of the demonic the merman would thus aspire to be the single individual who as the particular is higher than the universal.
(FT 123)

The demonic (which, as we have seen, is a sub-class of the aesthetic) lies outside the universal/ethical. The demonic person, just like the truly good person, must have great strength of character, because strength is required to remain in repulsion from or attached to 'the good'. It is a consistent position, a position which requires subjectivity and inwardness, but this inwardness is turned in on him or herself in rejection of God. This is an isolated position which cannot be achieved by going along with 'the crowd'.

If the person in the aesthetic stage rejects obligations to human beings, 'the demonic can also express itself in contempt for men ... his strength is his knowledge that he is better than all those who pass judgement on him (FT 131). The demonic is close to Nietzsche's superman – someone who thinks himself superior to those who pass judgement on him and who can ignore the demands of ethics and society which seek to constrain him. To such a person, both God and duty to human beings are essentially irrelevant – although for Kierkegaard the demonic establishes his identity by rejecting the divine, whereas Nietzsche can be interpreted as rejecting God entirely.

Another example would be the yuppie 'dealer' in the film *Wall Street* who considered that no moral rules applied to him – as far as he was concerned, in business 'anything goes', provided you are not caught.

Don Giovanni and Faust

The stories of Don Giovanni and Faust (which Kierkegaard discusses in *Fear and Trembling*) are apparently absurd, but they express something of great importance which Kierkegaard recognizes. Both Don Giovanni and Faust are in the demonic – that is why Don Giovanni refuses to repent of his crimes even when he is held by the Commendatore and is dragged off to hell. Both men define themselves against God and have so closed themselves off from God that they are unable to open themselves to the possibility of breaking out to overcome their state by relying on the divine. The choice lies between:

• maintenance of identity and being dragged to hell, *or*
• abandonment of the former identity by relying on God.

It is this latter step that Don Giovanni will not take. Effectively, such an individual cannot repent, as to do so means destroying the identity he or she has so painstakingly built up in opposition to and rejection of the divine.

Both Don Giovanni and Faust are individuals in that they have identified themselves by their rejection of God. They are extreme examples of the human effort to build individuality unaided. They do not drift with the crowd, they stand on their own – but they stand in opposition to the divine. They have turned themselves into the sort of people who are exiled from God and, in so doing, hell is the fate they have chosen. One of the key ingredients is *pride*: they have hung on in pride to their self-sufficiency and will not break out of it by relying, in humility, on God.

Don Giovanni is apparently not in despair, on the contrary he and Faust have a restless energy and zest for life – they represent the full force of the sensuous which is fleeing from anxiety. Ultimately, this energy and zest is grounded in the temporal which inevitably must have an end and it is when the barrenness of this is recognized that despair may result. Just before Don Giovanni is dragged off to hell, he stirs up within himself a renewed zest for life which represents his very identity. This is the furthest point he can reach: 'The situation consists in Don Giovanni being forced out to life's most extreme point' (Seducer's discourse on Don Giovanni). There he insists on staying – and he will go to hell holding fast to this position. He simply cannot bring himself to destroy the identity he has created for himself.

The demonic is the ultimate stage of anxiety which is found in the aesthetic stage. In its final analysis the only hope is to 'be saved by' God. The difference between the demonic and someone who has faith is that although both are in an absolute relationship to the absolute, the demonic is in a relationship of total rejection. The demonic establishes her or his identity in relation to the divine and by rejection of it.

Kierkegaard explains the demonic in terms of Christ's contact with the demoniac in the New Testament – the demoniac is anxious about the good, convinced that Christ has come to destroy him, and implores him to 'go away'. The definition of someone suffering the demonic form of anxiety comes from rejecting and defining themselves against the object of dread. There is, then, a relation to the divine; but a relation of repulsion. The demoniac is 'closed in' because this individual cannot bear to have his or her identity challenged by the divine.

5

The Ethical Stage

Judge William's rejection of the aesthetic in *Either/Or* is well-argued and cogent. In place of the aesthete's lack of commitment, the judge praises the freely chosen commitment that the ethical stage represents. It is by the individual's own choice of the ethical that he or she integrates the self and establishes his or her identity. The individual, the judge claims, makes a free decision to commit him or herself and then lives out this commitment. The individual is bound to freely chosen laws and God is not necessary. Judge William says:

> *The choice itself is crucial for the content of the personality; through the choice the personality submerges itself in that which is being chosen, and when it does not choose, it withers away in atrophy.*
> (EO 163)

Marriage as an Example of Ethical Choice

Marriage is the paradigm of choice. A woman and a man enter into a freely chosen commitment to each other and then live out this commitment. In place of the aesthete's approach of 'using' women with a total lack of commitment, the judge offers the high and honourable estate of marriage and freely chosen love based on duty. The judge praises women particularly in their role of wife and mother. This, he clearly considers, is the destiny of women, a message he continues to portray in *Stages on Life's Way*:

Woman is more beautiful as a bride than as a maiden; as mother she is more beautiful than as a bride. As mother she is a good word spoken at the right time, and she becomes more beautiful with the years.
(SLW 169)

The judge sees marriage as the paradigm of the ethical – acknowledged by society and of crucial importance to the community:

Marriage is and remains the most important journey of discovery a man can undertake. Every other kind of acquaintance with existence is superficial compared to that acquired by a married man – for he and he alone has thoroughly fathomed the depth of human existence.
(SLW 97)

It is important to recognize that Kierkegaard is not rejecting marriage in itself, he is rejecting the idea of finding one's identity through marriage or through any other conventional role. Everything in the ethical is open, disclosed and approved by the community; marriage and the raising of children are perfect examples of this. Married love, in the ethical stage, is a high calling and is to be contrasted with the fickleness of love in the aesthetic stage where there is no commitment. Marriage is not fickle as it is based on duty, it grows stronger with the passage of the years and the commitment shown to the public choice that was made in the marriage service. The judge admits that 'the first effervescent passion of falling in love' does not last, but marriage knows how to sustain this love (SLW 95). Marriage provides chains and bonds which, when freely accepted are not only welcome but also provide the identity for the married couple:

What I am through her she is through me, and neither of us is anything by oneself, but we are what we are in union. (SLW 93)

This is a good example of the role of the pseudonym in Kierkegaard's writings – this position rejects everything that Kierkegaard believed in, particularly the paramount importance of each person being a solitary individual before God. However, under the name of the pseudonym, Kierkegaard can delineate this possibility and argue for it; hoping, of course, that his reader will see its bankruptcy.

Love, according to this view, is essentially ethical duty – the duty to the freely chosen partner and to the children that result from the marriage. If the initial choice is strenuously maintained, as from an ethical point of view it must be, then this choice provides identity and meaning to the lives of the participants.

Baptism is another public ceremony in which the community puts its seal of approval on the birth of children. (When Kierkegaard was writing, of course, all children were baptized automatically just as everyone went to church each week; these were generally accepted social duties.) However, this easily becomes a substitute for the relationship with God which is essential:

> *A man and woman couple and nine months later an immortal soul is said to result which, with a sprinkle of water, becomes a Christian.*

Kierkegaard is not rejecting the importance of Christian baptism nor of marriage, but he is drawing attention to the danger of the outward ceremony being substituted for the inner transformation that is required. For Kierkegaard, Christianity is essentially an affair of spirit and affects one's inmost self – it cannot be expressed in terms of outer convention.

The Tragic Hero

It is not easy to live ethically, to live not according to desire but according to ethical rules. Kierkegaard, in *Fear and Trembling*, calls a man who does this and who is called to make supreme sacrifices for the sake of duty a 'Tragic Hero'. He cites the example of Agamemnon, Jephthah and Brutus – all of whom sacrifice the person they love to a higher ethical duty. Agamemnon, for instance, was the commander of the Greek fleet on the way to the siege of Troy when the fleet became becalmed. Lots were cast to determine who had brought this misfortune and the lot fell on Agamemnon's daughter. He had to sacrifice her for the good of his country. Someone who lives in the ethical lives according to rules which are understood but may still take great moral strength to live by: thus Agamemnon had to give up his ethical duty to his daughter for a higher ethical duty, namely his duty to his state. This moral strength comes from the individual concerned who refuses to give in to desire and instead does what is morally right.

Many Christians regard sin as acting immorally or unethically and would therefore see the ethical life as being the highest aim for a human being. This is not Kierkegaard's view. He considers this understanding to be essentially pagan, stemming from Aristotle. Thomas Aquinas used Aristotle's philosophy to lay down an ethical code which has become known as Natural Law and which forms the cornerstone of Catholic Natural Theology. On Aquinas' view, to sin is to act unethically: to act against morality is to act against reason and also against God. Kierkegaard rejected this: he considered that this involved no more than saying that duty to ethics was the same as duty to God and once one said this, then any idea that there really was a duty to God evaporated. All that was left was a duty to ethics.

As Kierkegaard's pseudonym Johannes de Silentio says in *Fear and Trembling*:

The whole of human existence is in that case entirely self-enclosed ...
God becomes an invisible, vanishing point, an impotent thought, and
his power is to be found only in the ethical ... (FT 96)

Putting ethics into central place led, Kierkegaard again considered, to despair – as he said:

> Every human existence not conscious of itself as spirit, or not personally conscious of itself before God as spirit, every human existence which is not grounded transparently in God, but opaquely rests or merges in some abstract universal [state, nation, etc.] or is in the dark about itself ... every such existence, however outstanding its accomplishments, however much it can account for even the whole of existence ... every such life is none the less despair. That is what the Old Church Fathers meant when they spoke of pagan virtues as splendid vices [Augustine, The City of God XIX.25]. They meant that the heart of paganism was despair, that the pagan was not conscious of himself before God as spirit. (SD 77)

Ethics and Conformity

For Kierkegaard, to live in the ethical is by no means the highest way of life. Indeed living the ethical life is all too often to lead a life of conformity, to conform oneself to the state, the community or, perhaps, Church – *but not to God*. You may be living a highly strenuous life, you may be morally admirable, you may never offend the moral code, but God is irrelevant. The attempt by one's own efforts to conform one's will to some chosen ethical norm ends in despair and in a denial of individuality because, essentially, what such a person does is to seek to conform him or herself to the community, the group, the crowd. He or she may well be praised, admired and understood, but only in finite terms.

This is a surprising conclusion as many Christians accept that sin is ethical wrongdoing and equate obedience to God with obedience to moral norms. They consider that the opposite of virtue is sin. Kierkegaard specifically says:

> ... *the opposite of sin is by no means virtue* ... *No, the opposite of sin is faith which is why in Romans 14:23 it says 'whosoever is not of faith, is sin'. And this is one of the most crucial definitions for the whole of Christianity: that the opposite of sin is not virtue but faith.*
> (SD 114–15)

The ethical with its personal choice of 'openness' and acceptance of society's values, even if these are regarded as being equivalent to a duty to God, is for Kierkegaard no more than a path through which one may realize the bankruptcy of trying to become close to God by 'keeping the rules'. Such an approach, as Jesus recognized in relation to the Jewish Torah, is doomed to failure. Recognition of this may open up the possibility for faith. For Kierkegaard, no individual self will be able to rest until it is in relationship with God rather than to temporal ends. However, recognizing this and realizing that one is in a state of 'unrest' and disquiet can lead a person onwards towards faith. We have seen that faith meant putting reason aside and accepting the Absolute Paradox, it means trusting in God in the absence of any proof. The life of faith is the life lived in relationship with God and, in *Either/Or*, Kierkegaard through his pseudonym is effectively trying to lead his reader to see that the ethical life as well as the aesthetic will end in disappointment.

There are a variety of implicit pointers to this in the text when Judge William, while writing to the aesthetic Seducer and praising the virtues of the ethical, also warns of the dangers of having anything to do with truly religious categories. Real faith is, for the judge, too impossibly strenuous, too lonely, too costly a path. The virtuous ethical life may require dedication but it is, essentially, a safe path which reason can understand and which everyone can applaud and appreciate.

Marriage, by contrast, although it may involve ethical striving, nevertheless also provides comfort and security. Ibsen's play *A Doll's House*, was probably based on Kierkegaard's work (as was Ibsen's *Brand*, which illustrates the absolute nature of the 'all or nothing' demand) and illustrates well the denial of individuality and individual development that marriage often involves. Kierkegaard does not have a high view of marriage – this does not mean that he considers that marriage is incompatible with Christianity, but that it can only be compatible if the two parties are both true individuals.

Too often, Kierkegaard considers, the demands of society and conformity, the social expectations that come from raising children, setting up home and the like become a substitute for individuality and the God-relationship. This he sees as a travesty of the Christian demand. He blames priests for this and the general wish for mediocrity – there is a demand by 'the crowd', the mass of people, to be able to live an ordinary, unexamined and passionless life in which God is essentially irrelevant and yet they want this life to be regarded as Christian. Such a person comes to the end of his life and 'one thing had escaped him; his consciousness has taken no note of God' (CUP 219).

Either/Or is essentially a negative book, although it does not appear like this. Kierkegaard uses his pseudonym to point to the ultimate bareness of both the aesthetic and the ethical, leaving the way open for what Kierkegaard effectively considers is the true end for every human being – the religious.

The Individual before God

Many contemporary philosophers and, indeed, theologians see ethical obligation to the community as higher than the religious. Kierkegaard considers the ethical stage to be dangerous precisely because it is the category of the crowd, the community. All too easily, the ethical may become the category which will not allow a person to attain individuality. Kierkegaard is outright in his condemnation of anyone who thinks they can approach God as a member of a club or group – essentially, Christianity is a matter of inwardness and therefore the concern of each individual.

Although some may reject his or her activities, the aesthete is at least trying to be an individual and, as such, may be brought to the point of despair where he or she is faced with two alternatives – to remain locked into him or herself or to submit humbly to God. It is this possible and decisive transition from despair to faith which, for Kierkegaard, is most important of all. The person in the aesthetic may be closer to God than the ethical individual because he or she at least is alone and isolated and has begun to take him or herself seriously – this, in turn, may lead to despair and the need for faith. Despair is possible in both the ethical and the aesthetic stages, but it is easier for the ethical to provide an apparent and illusory security (Tolstoy's short book 'The Death of Ivan Illich' is a good example of this).

Judge William portrays a complacency and confidence in the ethical choices he has made that was anathema to Kierkegaard; only as an individual, alone and isolated from the crowd, can true identity be found. Despair may finally pull the individual to her or his true home – which can only be found through the 'small gate' of humility and trust in the eternal. *Either/Or* is designed to bring its reader to see the bankruptcy of both the aesthetic and the ethical in order to help the readers not to waste their lives. As Kierkegaard puts it (my emphasis):

So much is spoken about wasting one's life. *But the only wasted life is the life of one who has so lived it, deceived by life's pleasures or its sorrows, that he never became decisively, eternally, conscious of himself as spirit, as self, or, what is the same, he never became aware – and gained in the deepest sense the impression – that there is a God there and that 'he' himself, his self, exists before this God ...* **So many live their lives in this way ... when the hour glass has run out, the hour glass of temporality, when the worldly tumult is silenced and the restless or unavailing urgency comes to an end, when all about you is still as it is in eternity – whether you are man or woman, rich or poor, dependent or free, happy or**

unhappy ... eternity asks you and every one of these millions of millions just one thing: whether you have lived in despair or not ... (SD 57-8)

Despair at the attempt to attain an identity by one's own efforts is the step before faith. *Either/Or* presents us with dead ends – the individual can only move beyond these dead ends by willing one thing: to belong to Christ. It is in this stage that Kierkegaard's comments about women can be seen in their true perspective – his negative comments only reflect what he saw as a truth: that most women and men do waste and fritter away their lives. However, if they can be brought to see beyond this, the distinctions of gender vanish:

> In the relationship to God, where ... a distinction between man and woman vanishes, it is the case both for the man and the woman that self-abandonment is the self, and that the self is acquired through self abandonment. (SD 80-1)

Before God, human beings are individuals. This is the great equality and it is only before God that all outward distinctions vanish – a theme Kierkegaard continually takes up in *Works of Love*.

6

The Religious Stage

The aesthetic and the ethical stages both end in despair. The person in the ethical stage has made his own choice of an ethical end in order to create an identity for himself and thus will, like the aesthete, end in despair, as the ethical choice will come to be realized as simply a construct and one can never achieve compliance with the ethical 'good' by one's own efforts.

Only when this despair is reached and when it is understood that all finite ends terminate in disappointment may the individual come to relate him or herself directly to God. Human beings learn to live behind the mask or cloak of public opinion and think that this gives them identity and security. Only when this is recognized, in Kierkegaard's view, is the way open for the individual to take the religious dimension seriously.

The religious stage entails a personal relationship with God and a direct accountability to God – all finite ends are put in second place. Two steps are involved in the religious stage: firstly the subordination of all temporal ends, and secondly the focusing of the whole of an individual's existence on the relation to the eternal. The second step involves the individual having an absolute relationship to the absolute or, as Kierkegaard puts it, 'acting absolutely towards absolute ends and relatively towards relative ends'.

If only the first step is taken, despair will again result. Resignation from all temporal concerns can be achieved by an individual's own efforts – such an individual is a 'knight of infinite resignation', who surrenders all temporal aspirations and, in so doing, becomes conscious of being an individual before the eternal – an 'eternal consciousness' comes into being when she or he becomes aware of God free from the distractions of the temporal. However, the second step is the step of faith and, as we saw in Chapter 2, faith involves an action by God. It is not something that can be achieved simply by an act of will. What is more, humility is an essential precondition for faith.

It is only when one is broken by despair, unable to rely on one's self and one's own strength that real faith can arise. This is why despair is so important as an essential precondition for faith. The person who is strong, doing well in the world and self-sufficient will not come to faith. Pride and self-sufficiency are effective barriers to a relationship with God.

Kierkegaard maintains that the religious stage requires all worldly concerns (the temporal) to be put into second place to centring one's life on God. This does not mean becoming a hermit, rather it involves living in such a way that temporal matters are not of primary concern. Someone who takes this step may become materially comfortable and even be successful, but this will not be important or significant to them – if they were all lost it would be of no significance. Kierkegaard gives an example of Job who loses everything and, gradually, comes to accept this. He regains the temporal trappings that he once lost but these are no longer of primary significance to him.

Kierkegaard takes seriously the biblical assertion that, for God, what is not thinkable, what is least expected is possible – but only through faith. Faith is always non-rational, it 'begins precisely where thought stops' (CUP 412).

Suffering is a mark of the God-relationship – if someone really puts God into first place then this will inevitably lead to confrontation with the world and misunderstanding by others. This isolation is uncomfortable and lonely; to sustain the faith journey through the whole of one's life is precisely the task but it is incredibly arduous. It is much more 'sensible', much more 'rational', much more understandable and acceptable to conform, but this is precisely a denial of the God-relationship:

The ethical constitutes the temptation; the God-relationship has come into being; the immanence of ethical despair has been broken through ... (CUP 235)

However, to sustain the God-relationship, day by day, week by week and year by year is demanding, and few people will be willing to take the lonely path that this involves. Just as being in love is a one-to-one relationship, so relating oneself wholly to God is something that can be done only between the individual and God. No one can relate to God by conforming to the crowd.

The established order, Kierkegaard considered, represented the accepted ethical and other conventions of modern society or even the Church. This established order is certain to be offended and to reject Jesus because his message is too uncomfortable and because he challenges the supremacy of reason. Those who live their lives by conforming to the expectations of their peers will also be offended:

'Why', says the established order, 'why do you want to plague and tor-ture yourself with the prodigious measuring rod of the ideal? Have recourse to the established order, attach yourself to it. There is the measure. If you are a student, then you can be sure that the Professor is the measure and the truth; if you are a parson, then the Bishop is the way and the life; if you are a scrivener, the Judge is the standard ... The established order is the rational; and you are fortunate if you occupy the position of relativity accorded you – and for the rest let your colleagues take care of ...' 'Do you mean to say my salvation?' 'Why certainly. If with regard to this matter you encounter in the end some obstacle, can you not be contented like all the others, when your last hour has come, to go well baled and crated in one of the large ship-ments which the established order sends straight through to heaven under its own seal ...' (TC 91)

The established order of the Church maintains that provided one is a Christian as it understands it (possibly by baptism, confirmation, occasional church attendance and giving money regularly to the Church to sustain the standard of living of the priests) then this is all that is required. Secure as a member of the club, each individual will be shipped straight off to heaven after death. Kierkegaard thinks that this makes a mockery of God – each individual, on his view, must render personal account for her or his life. Faithfulness to the God-relationship and how this has been lived out on a daily basis will be the basis for the judgement of God.

It is now possible to see the different approaches to love represented by the three stages:

- in the aesthetic, love is essentially sensual or erotic and the person uses love to maximize her or his enjoyment. The purpose is to be loved and to enjoy this experience.
- in the ethical stage, love is essentially duty and is represented by freely chosen love within the family.
- in the religious, however, love is focused primarily on God and, because of that, on love of neighbour – it is a giving love. For Kierkegaard, a religious love is essentially *a non-preferential love* that does not favour any one human being against others.

Kierkegaard does not consider that the religious stage rules out the sexual – but he does consider that the sexual is such a powerful force that it can easily lead people away from the eternal. As he puts it:

> *Here, as everywhere, I must decline every misunderstood conclusion, as if, for instance, the true task should now be to abstract from the sexual, i.e. in an outward sense to annihilate it ... The task, of course, is to bring it under the qualification of the spirit (here lie all the moral problems of the erotic) ...* (CA 80)

The problem, in other words, is how, if one lives a life centred on God, one can subsume sexual relationships under this category without the love that such relationships express becoming preferential.

Religion A and Religion B

Although, as outlined above, the religious stage is the third of three stages, in fact Kierkegaard analyses two distinct segments of the Religious Stage – Religion A and Religion B. Religion A is outlined above: the individual recognizes the bankruptcy of the aesthetic and ethical, subordinates the temporal and looks to Christ as the prototype of the perfect human being, not as a personal saviour. The individual, by an act of will, renounces the temporal in order to make room for the eternal. The individual can take the step from the aesthetic or ethical to Religion A when the barrenness of the temporal is recognized, however the step into Religion B cannot be made unaided. Gregor Malantschuk describes the step into Religion A as:

> ... away with human self-reliance to risk oneself upon 'the seventy thousand fathoms' of water. This daring act is the beginning of the journey on the religious way. (MALANTSCHUK, KIERKEGAARD'S WAY TO THE TRUTH, REITZEL, 56).

There is, however, nothing specifically Christian in Religion A and it is the decisively Christian categories that are found in Religion B with, in particular, the introduction of the idea of sin. The focus of Religion B is the Absolute Paradox of the God-Man which requires the abandonment of the supremacy of reason as well as of the security found in the objective – it necessarily involves, therefore, the enormous risk of staking one's life on something which may be mistaken. Religion B is characterized by vulnerability as well as by an awareness of sin and the acceptance of forgiveness.

Sin is not a popular word today but for Kierkegaard it was central. An individual can understand the rate of progress on the road towards God by looking at the extent to which there is a consciousness of sin. The further down the road the individual travels, the greater will be the consciousness of failure before God and total dependence on God's love. All security is left behind, the individual's own strength is abandoned and he or she lives by faith alone. Nowhere is faith greater than belief in the forgiveness of sins which is an absolutely essential part of Christian faith. Faith is the condition necessary for the forgiveness of sins – Kierkegaard claims that people lightly skip over the idea of forgiveness, but such people do not take the relationship with God or the eternal seriously. To those that do, forgiveness is nothing less than a miracle. An individual is bound by individual action into the power of sin and it is God's action in the incarnation that is the crucial event in freeing this power.

There are forces acting to push and pull the individual into faith. First is despair, which can push the individual towards God. The individual may come, through despair in the ethical or aesthetic stages, to recognize that it is only in relation to God that any security and hope can be found. Secondly, God, on the other side, provides the gift of grace. Kierkegaard was adamant, however, that 'cheap grace' must be rejected – grace comes only when the individual is broken and in pieces, it is not an automatic 'freebie', given out like sweets to children. It is true that Kierkegaard considers grace to be a universal gift – but it is one that has to be accepted by the individual.

In Chapter 2 we saw that the opposite of faith was offence and offence is itself sinful. This is why the opposite of sin is not virtue but faith. Someone who cannot accept the forgiveness of sin is, essentially, someone who rejects the incarnation and this makes sin still worse. The individual chooses to remain in sin and rejects the paradox because it does not make sense (SD 113–24). She or he is offended by the Christian message and continues to give reason primacy. Kierkegaard is firm in rejecting all objective certainty with regard to Christianity's truth; this is particularly to leave room for faith and the gift of grace by God:

> ... *depart from me, damned assurance! Save me, O God, from ever becoming absolutely certain. Preserve me in the hinterland of uncertainty so that it may always be absolutely certain that if I attain salvation I receive it by grace.* (ED 218)

Religion A can be attained by an individual's own efforts. A person can will to give up all hope of the temporal and to ground themselves in the Eternal. They can look to Christ as an exemplar but the transition from A to B occurs when the individual realizes that her or his own will is not sufficient and depends on Christ alone for forgiveness of sins and for salvation.

Faith and Discipleship

Faith for Kierkegaard is the highest – which is why he was so angry with philosophers, priests and theologians who attempt to defraud people out of that which is highest of all. It is very tempting for the individual to avoid the suffering that faith will bring and the commitment it entails, but faith is made more difficult by the ridicule and opposition of the crowd. Faith requires, therefore, isolation – it necessarily involves a lonely path walking hand in hand with God alone and relying and trusting on God for the whole of one's life. It involves accepting being loved when one is acutely conscious of how unlovable one is.

Kierkegaard's pseudonym, Johannes Climacus, seeks to work out step by step (the name Johannes Climacus is taken from the Egyptian monk of this name who wrote *The Ladder of Divine Ascent*), using philosophic reasoning, what faith amounts to. For Kierkegaard this is a particularly masculine way of proceeding and is to be contrasted with the way of love. He puts it like this:'... women's whole life is love ... [Johannes Climacus'] whole life was thinking'.

Johannes Climacus' delight was to begin with a single thought and then, by coherent thinking, to climb step by step to a higher one, because to him coherent thinking was an ascent to paradise. He was a rational, male philosopher investigating Christian faith and giving an account of it. Nowhere could there be a clearer statement of Kierkegaard's distance from his pseudonym. For Kierkegaard himself, philosophy and language in general can only serve to bring us to a place where words come to an end and when, as individuals, we are confronted by God. Love may be an expression of the confrontation but we will not arrive at the ability to love through philosophy.

Faith is, essentially, a life – a life lived in imitation of Christ and as a follower of Christ. It involves becoming a self, an individual whose life is informed by an awareness of dependence on and accountability to God. The 'admirer' of Christ is not the follower; admirers can look on Christ objectively, they may talk about Christ, they may applaud him – but their admiration does not lead to following him on a day-to-day basis. Only the follower is the disciple. Kierkegaard puts this well in his parable 'Luther's Return', in which Luther comes back and challenges a religious writer (Kierkegaard may well have been thinking of himself here):

> ... Assume that Luther has risen from the grave ... assume that one day he addresses me and says 'Are you a believer? Do you have faith?' Everyone who knows me as an author will recognize that I am the one who comes out best from such an examination for I constantly said 'I have not faith' ... However, I will not lay stress on this; for as all others call themselves Christians and believers, I also will say 'Yes, I am also a believer'. 'How is that?' replies Luther 'for I have not noticed anything in you, and yet I have watched your life; and you know faith is a perturbing thing. To what effect has faith, which you say you have, perturbed you? Where have you witnessed for the truth and

where against untruth? What sacrifices have you made, what persecutions have you endured for Christianity?'. My reply: 'I can protest to you that I have faith'. 'Protest, protest – what sort of talk is that ... Bah, an end to this nonsense. What avails your protestation?' 'Yes, but if you would read some of my books, you will see how I have described faith, so I know therefore I must have it ' ... 'I believe the fellow is mad! If it is true that you know how to describe faith, it only proves that you are a poet, and if you can describe it well, it proves that you are a good poet; but that is very far from proving that you are a believer. Perhaps you can also weep in describing faith, that would then prove that you are a good actor'. (FSE 42–3)

7

Ethics, Sin and the Relationship to God

In previous chapters we have seen that Kierkegaard considered that Christianity was based on the claim that Jesus was fully God and fully human, a claim which went against reason. He considered that this depends on the individual's subjective acceptance of the truth claim of Christianity and development of a relationship to God. The religious stage of life involved the solitary individual staking the whole of her or his existence on this. Both the aesthetic and the ethical stages in life ended in despair and it is only in the religious stage that an individual's real identity and eternal destiny could be found. This picture, however, raises an important issue, namely if the ethical is not the highest then it is possible for a faith relationship with God to call an individual outside the ethical. Kierkegaard discusses this in *Fear and Trembling* (whose pseudonymous author is Johannes de Silentio) which is a detailed analysis of the biblical story of Abraham and Isaac.

It is not altogether clear what Kierkegaard means by ethics in this context. In Kierkegaard's Denmark, the philosophy of Hegel dominated, although the influence of Immanuel Kant was still strong. According to Kant,

> ... *even though something is represented as being commanded by God ... yet, if it flatly contradicts morality, it cannot, despite all appearances, be of God (for instance were a father ordered to kill his son ...).* (KANT, RELIGION WITHIN THE LIMITS OF REASON ALONE, TR. GREENE AND HUDSON, 81)

For Hegel, morality is that which is for the good of society as a whole – ethics is concerned with the good of all human beings and not with the individual in relationship to God. Indeed, Kierkegaard quotes Hegel as going so far as to say that to have the limited outlook of a single individual is 'a moral form of evil' and to remain in this state is to be in 'sin or in a state of temptation ...' (FT 83)

If duty to God is no more than duty to ethics, then, Kierkegaard maintains, all that is happening effectively is that ethical duty is being given a new name. As we have seen in Chapter 5, many Christian thinkers follow Aquinas' use of Aristotle in basing their view of ethics on Natural Law. This assumes that reason can arrive at what is the *telos*, the purpose or destiny of human beings, and that reason can differentiate between the real and apparent good. This view, adopted particularly by the Roman Catholic Church, rejects any idea of a specifically Christian ethic and instead maintains that it is possible to arrive at Natural Law which is valid for all people at all times.

Essentially, on this view, there is no such thing as a direct duty by the individual to God and one's duty is entirely expressed in ethics which is mediated by the Church community and those in authority. Certainly it would be impossible for God to demand of an individual something which clearly contravened ethical norms – yet this, Kierkegaard claims, is precisely the situation portrayed in the story of Abraham and Isaac.

The Faith of Abraham

In the Book of Genesis, God commands Abraham to sacrifice his son, Isaac, even though God has previously promised Abraham that through Isaac he would have innumerable descendants. Genesis records God's command as follows:

God tested Abraham, and said to him ... 'Take your son, your only son Isaac, whom you love, and go to the land of Moriah, and offer him there as a burnt offering upon one of the mountains of which I shall tell you.' (GENESIS 22:1–2)

Some modern biblical commentators hold that the Abraham and Isaac story is fictitious – the story was inserted as a prohibition against child sacrifice and was never seen as a test of Abraham's faith. Kierkegaard could admit this possibility, although he never himself took this position. What he does is to explore the implications of this story – and it must be remembered that, for Christians, Abraham is held up in the New Testament as an idealized figure of faith, so that from a theological point of view he cannot be dismissed that easily. Kierkegaard sees Abraham as the paradigm of an individual who put obedience of God in first place and everything else, including his ethical obligations, in second place.

The highest ethical obligation that a father can have is to his child, and Isaac was the son of Abraham's old age, loved by Abraham above everything in the world. When God called Abraham to sacrifice Isaac, God was asking the unreasonable, the irrational: after all, it was God himself who had promised that, through Isaac, Abraham would have innumerable descendants. How, then, could God command the death of Isaac? Abraham's response was to trust God and to do what God commanded – even though he could not understand.

Abraham set out to sacrifice Isaac and *at the same time continued to believe in God's promise.* The philosopher will, of course, say that this does not make sense: if Isaac is killed, then Isaac cannot be the source of innumerable descendants. Abraham's faith, however, went beyond what could be justified by reason: he trusted God even though he could not make sense of his faith. He trusted that he would be 'the father of many nations' and that this would be fulfilled through his only Son by his wife, Sarah: 'through Isaac shall your descendants be named' (GENESIS 21:12).

It may be argued that Abraham has grounds for his faith and his response is not as absurd as Kierkegaard would have it appear – Abraham's obedience to God was not an isolated instance; his whole life had been based on love for and trust in God. He had left Ur of the Chaldees on God's instruction; he had parted from Lot on God's command; his wife had conceived long after the menopause because of God's intervention. Nevertheless, Kierkegaard's point is that Abraham behaves against ethical rules and Kierkegaard's real concern is not to discuss an old story but to examine the relevance this story has for today.

Beyond Ethics

Either Abraham was a true knight of faith – or he was deluded. The person who says that the ethical is the highest must maintain the latter, whilst Kierkegaard maintains the former. Essentially he is saying that it is possible for a command from God to call the individual beyond ethics. Normally, it is a temptation to move outside ethics: ethics considers that it is supreme and if anyone acts against the demands of ethics, then he or she sins and ethics will condemn him or her and insist on repentance and conformity with the ethical. As we have already seen, the ethical stage may be demanding, but essentially it is 'safe' – everyone can understand and admire ethical behaviour and everyone will be quick to condemn and disapprove of those who infringe the demands of ethics. Kierkegaard's question is whether it is possible for a person to be called outside the demands of ethics and not be in sin.

If the religious stage is a possibility, then it may be possible to be called outside the frontiers of ethics into the religious – in this case, the relationship with God may call an individual to put the demands of this relationship into first place and to ignore conventional ethics. Kierkegaard's point is that this is a conceptual possibility and, if this is the case, then it may be a temptation to continue to abide by the demands of ethics. In other words, if God calls you to act in a certain way and if reason, convention, the demands of the community or an individual's own sense of what is 'appropriate' proclaim this as 'wrong' or 'mistaken', then to give into these demands is itself a temptation. As an example, St Francis publicly repudiated his father outside Assisi Cathedral. He had an ethical duty of obedience to his father but he rejected this in favour of what he considered to be a higher calling from God.

Following the command from God, Abraham is portrayed as setting out for Mount Moriah. His love for Isaac remains unchanged, what he sets out to do is undertaken solely in obedience to God:

> *The absolute duty can then lead to what ethics would forbid, but it can by no means make the knight of faith have done with loving.* (FT 101)

As he sets out his love for his son is unchanged and he does not tell anyone what he is about to do. He does not tell his wife, nor his servants, nor his son – how could he? They would all have tried to prevent him and regarded him as mad. Silence is forced on the person who enters the religious stage and here again there is a contrast with Hegelian ethics:

> *The Hegelian philosophy assumes there is no justified concealment ... it is therefore consistent in its requirement of disclosure.* (FT 109)

Ethics rejects the idea of secrecy whereas both the aesthetic and the religious require secrecy and silence but they are essentially different. Abraham *cannot* speak because nothing he can say will make him understood (FT 137). Abraham is the paradigm of the person for whom language no longer serves as a means of communication. Unlike the Tragic Hero (see Chapter 5) who is called on by ethics to sacrifice one ethical duty for another, Abraham has no higher ethical objective; he does not act to benefit his community or his family. He is in absolute isolation. People can understand and admire the Tragic Hero – but who, Kierkegaard asks, can understand Abraham? He is called on to put into second place that which he loves most in the world, his son. Not only that, but Abraham is called to act against reason. God has, after all, promised Abraham that, through Isaac, he will have innumerable descendants – yet God commands Abraham to kill Isaac. This does not make sense: it can only appear to Abraham as if God is denying his original promise. Abraham, however, has faith: he trusts God even though he cannot understand and Abraham regards his duty to God as the highest duty.

Kierkegaard's pseudonym Johannes Climacus asks why Abraham acts against ethics. His answer is clear: 'For God's sake, and what is exactly the same, for his own' (FT 88).

Teleological Suspension of the Ethical

Kierkegaard considers that there can be such a thing as the teleological suspension of the ethical. In other words, ethics may be put into second place because an individual has a higher *telos* or end – namely a relationship with God. A duty to God can, therefore, call someone beyond the frontiers of ethics in response to a command from God. If this is not the case, then Abraham is mad or deluded. Only if there is the possibility of an absolute duty to God is it possible to make sense of Abraham's action in setting out to sacrifice Isaac.

Ethics has a safety and security that is not available to anyone who leaves it behind and once the security of the ethical is abandoned then the individual faces a real danger – is he or she in fact being obedient to God or is he or she mad or deluded? One mark of sanity may be an ability to ask oneself whether or not one is mad. Kierkegaard fully recognizes the danger of delusion and accepts that there is no easy way to determine who is the person of faith and who is the fanatic. Ethics will condemn them both because of their secrecy and will insist that both conform their wills to its dictates. Again this emphasizes the loneliness of the path taken by the person who really tries to live in a subjective relationship with God – there is no security, no certainty, no objective test. The individual is alone, dependent on faith and with the knowledge that it is always at least possible that he or she could be mistaken. This is a position of extreme vulnerability. It would be far safer and more secure to abandon this relationship to God and instead to conform to the demands of the Church or other community in which we live. After all, these can be widely understood and the person who lives in the ethical sphere will be respected and admired. The religious stage has no such security.

Kierkegaard is careful to separate the demands of the Church as recognized and accepted by society (which he terms 'Christendom') and the demands of God. Too often, he maintains, the demands of God are abandoned by priests and Church leaders who instead substitute demands that are comfortable and simply involve conformity with accepted standards of behaviour. The scandal of the gospel is done away with and the offence of the Absolute Paradox is eliminated.

There are two separate issues here:

(1) Is it possible for a duty to God to suspend one's duty to ethics? Kierkegaard deals with this in Problema II (FT 96 ff.) which is entitled 'Is there an absolute duty to God?'. He concludes this section as follows:

> ... either there is an absolute duty to God, and if so then it is the paradox that the single individual as the particular is higher than the universal and as the particular stands in an absolute relation to the absolute – or else faith has never existed because it has existed always; or else Abraham is done for ... (FT 108)

In other words if there is no such thing as an absolute duty to God which can suspend ethical duty, then 'faith' is merely compliance with ethics and has no distinctive role.

(2) How does one know that what one considers to be a call from God is genuine and not a delusion? Kierkegaard rejects any easy answer to his question and maintains that it is always possible to be mistaken.

The difficulty of determining (2) does not, however, rule out (1) as being a live possibility and Kierkegaard clearly maintains that a duty to God can suspend ethical norms.

Abraham, of course, is a paradigm case: yet Kierkegaard considers that knights of faith exist in every age. However, they will not be immediately visible, they are concealed. They will look exactly like ordinary men and women. Nothing external may be detectable, this is because the essential quality of the knight of faith is interior. No outsider can claim that someone else is or is not a knight of faith; the simple person as much as the clever may be a knight of faith. Faith, for Kierkegaard, is the great equalizer — the one thing that every human being can have in common no matter what their background or circumstances.

Silence and an absence of words are essential to Kierkegaard's understanding of a life lived in relationship with God — yet he himself is aware of a tension here as he expends great effort and many words in trying to help people to understand what the faith relationship requires. He is using words to force people into silence and a consideration of self. Communication with others usually involves blunting the challenge imposed by living with God. As Kierkegaard says: 'Silence in the relationship to God is invigorating ... talking about one's God-relationship is an emptying that weakens' (J 3988). This is why he stresses indirect communication — people have to be brought to see something — the reality of which words cannot grasp.

It is significant that in the area of a direct, individual relationship with God, the possibility of secrecy and acting against Church teaching Kierkegaard differs markedly from Augustine, Aquinas and other theologians. Richard Price in his book *Augustine* (Great Christian Thinkers series) quotes his subject as saying: 'Each person is to think the same about his soul. Let each man hate to have a feeling he cannot share with others'.

Kierkegaard considers that a call from God may enforce silence on an individual and may call such a person outside both ethical and generally accepted Christian norms. Augustine sees Christianity as essentially a communal affair both in the Church on earth and with the saints in heaven. Kierkegaard instead emphasizes the individual faith journey and the priority of the individual in relation to God. Kierkegaard does not reject community, but he does consider that genuine community can only be found amidst people who have first become individuals.

8

The Truth of the God-Relationship

Kierkegaard did not consider that there were any outward signs which could enable one person to determine whether another was or was not genuinely living in a God-relationship. This relationship was subjective and could not be measured in objective terms. One of his concerns was to hold a mirror before his reader to enable the individual to decide whether he or she is in a genuine God-relationship. *Purity of Heart is to will one thing* is Kierkegaard's great spiritual classic. It is particularly significant because it is written under his own name and also it is dedicated to 'That Solitary Individual' which was the highest category that Kierkegaard outlined. A solitary individual is an individual living life before God and it is to this state that Kierkegaard himself aspired. The book is based on the Letter of James, Chapter 4, verse 8:

Draw near to God and he will draw near to you. Cleanse your hands you sinners, and purify your hearts you double-minded. (PH 53)

Purity of Heart is stated to be a 'Spiritual Preparation for the office of Confession'. Kierkegaard never specifically states that 'the one thing' which he calls his reader to will is the God-relationship, but this is clear from the text and from other books, for instance:

Now the question is, Wilt thou be offended or wilt thou believe? If thou wilt believe, then thou must pass through the possibility of offence, accept Christianity on any terms ... So, a fig for the understanding! So you say, 'Whether it now is a help or a torment, I will one thing only. I will belong to Christ, I will be a Christian.' (TC 117)

For Kierkegaard, this is the essential test for someone who wishes to be a Christian – whether she or he, with passion and total inner conviction, will stake everything on the desire to belong to Christ, to live in relationship with God and to place God at the centre of the whole of life.

'If there is something eternal in a man,' says Kierkegaard, 'it must be able to exist and to be grasped within every change' (PH 36). The individual's relationship to the eternal does not depend on any outer factors: neither youth nor age, poverty or wealth, sickness or health, worldly success or failure. The individual should never outgrow the eternal and only the eternal is always relevant and is always present no matter what the outer circumstances. The presence of the eternal

... is like the murmuring of a brook. If you go buried in your own thoughts, if you are busy, then you do not notice it at all in passing. You are not aware that this murmuring exists. But if you stand still, then you discover it. And if you have discovered it, then you must stand still. And when you stand still, then it persuades you. And when it has persuaded you, then you must stoop and listen to it attentively. And when you have stooped to listen to it, then it captures you ... (PH 49)

In prayer, God does not get to know something, but the person praying gets to know something about him or herself. Prayer does not change God, it changes the person uttering it. Kierkegaard maintains that in prayer we learn something and the refusal to learn about ourselves is the greatest possible loss:

... there is an ignorance that no one need be troubled by, if he was deprived either of the opportunity or the capacity to learn. But there is an ignorance about one's own life that is equally tragic for the learned and the simple, for both are bound by the same responsibility. This ignorance is called self-deceit ... The ignorant man can gradually acquire wisdom and knowledge, but the self-deluded one if he won 'the one thing needful' would have won purity of heart. (PH 52)

For Kierkegaard, then, purity of heart involves 'knowing yourself' but, unlike the god Apollo whose catch-phrase this was, for Kierkegaard it means knowing oneself before God:

... Purity of Heart is the very wisdom that is acquired through prayer. A man of prayer does not pore over learned books for he is the wise man 'whose eyes are opened' – when he kneels down. (PH 55)

For Kierkegaard, repentance and remorse for sin are both important – they are guides to deepening the individual's understanding of self in relation to God and must not simply be passed over quickly. An individual needs to reflect on his or her failings and on what changes to self are needed – the individual must be self-conscious or conscious of self. Precipitate repentance is false (PH 44), and one needs to reflect on one's failings in order to understand better the sort of person one is in contrast to the sort of person one needs to become. This is not a matter of guilt but of re-orientation. Hence a time of preparation for confession is important. One's 'sin' or one's failings in fact reflect a failure to will sufficiently passionately the 'one thing' that Kierkegaard considers to be paramount. 'Sin' is not a question of acting immorally, it is a much deeper concept which entails a failure of passion or love in relation to God.

To 'will one thing' is to will to be 'that single individual' and to live your life wholly in relationship to God. This is the only thing that can be singular and is not 'double-minded', being mixed with a variety of alternative motives. All temporal objectives, whether they be power, money, reputation, security, marriage, children or happiness are multiple and cannot be the 'one thing' that stays constant in every single situation in life. There are many temptations which call the individual away from willing one thing – including the temptation to aim for what is impressive instead of the relationship with God. In particular, there are barriers that get in the way of this single-minded concentration on living in relationship with God, and Kierkegaard identifies these as follows:

(I) THE REWARD-DISEASE

Someone who falls under this heading may start out willing to live in a relationship with God and may, with enthusiasm, continue for a time. However, then he faces opposition and although at first he never desired to be rewarded in this world, he found it too difficult to keep it up. Gradually, therefore, he let go of his concentration on God and instead sought approval from others: he could not stand their opposition or the loneliness that comes from willing one thing single-mindedly so he ended up relating himself to the temporal world and forgetting the eternal.

(II) WILLING THE GOOD OUT OF FEAR OF PUNISHMENT

The punishment Kierkegaard has in mind here may be punishment from other human beings or punishment from God. For Kierkegaard, the fear of God is the beginning of wisdom. People often talk of the love of God and ridicule anyone who actually lives his or her life in fear and respect for God. As he puts it:

> ... spiritually understood there is a ruinous illness, namely, not to fear what a man should fear; the sacredness of modesty, God in the heavens, the command of duty, the voice of conscience, the accountability of eternity ... (PH 80)

'The fear of God' is not the same as 'fear of punishment'. Duty to God is, for Kierkegaard, an absolute – a categorical duty undertaken for itself alone and not for any other reason. Fear of punishment is something else. A person who fears punishment:

> ... does not will the Good, he wills it only out of fear of punishment. Therefore – if there were no punishment! In that 'if' lurks double-mindedness. If there were no punishment! In that 'if' hisses double-mindedness. (PH 83)

In other words such a person is only seeking God out of fear (whether it be fear of other people or of eternal punishment). If the fear of punishment was removed the person would no longer seek God. Such a person is double-minded. Fear is:

> ... a dry nurse for the child; it has no milk; a blood-less corrector for the youth; it has no beckoning Encouragement; a niggardly disease for the adult; it has no blessing; a horror for the aged ... (PH 85)

It is not possible to develop a love relationship with God where the primary motive is fear. To claim that this is possible is to be double-minded. Love seeks no reward and has no motive. Kierkegaard considers that the world has no power over an individual who is truly trying to 'will one thing':

> To be sure the world has power. It can lay many a burden upon the innocent one. It can make his life sour and laborious for him. It can rob him of his life. But it cannot punish an innocent one. How wonderful, here is a limit, a limit that is invisible ... When the good man stands on the other side of the boundary line inside the fortification of eternity, he is strong, stronger than the whole world ... (PH 97–8)

This strength is based on a love relationship which is not driven by any alternative motive other than the relationship itself.

(III) EGOCENTRIC SERVICE OF THE GOOD

This 'barrier' to willing one thing occurs with the person who wills that 'the Good' should triumph in the world, but he wills that the triumph should be through him. He is essentially self-centred and feeds on the feeling of pride that his success engenders:

> When a man is active early and late 'For the sake of the Good', storming about noisily and restlessly, hurling himself into time, as a sick man throws off his clothes, scornful of the world's reward; when such a man makes a place among men, then the masses think what he himself imagines, that he is inspired ... he wishes to sacrifice all, he fears nothing, only he will not sacrifice himself in daily self-forgetfulness. This he fears to do. (PH 101;103)

Kierkegaard considers that God does not 'need' human beings and the conceit that God does need a particular individual so that God's purposes may succeed is, in fact, merely human pride at work. The idea that one is 'needed' by God is, essentially, egocentricity, and this is the *real* motive for the individual's action. Such a person is not being single-minded in trying to relate to God, he or she is sub-consciously feeding their ego.

(IV) COMMITMENT TO A CERTAIN DEGREE

'At bottom,' Kierkegaard says, 'this is the way all double-mindedness expresses itself' (PH 106). In trade or commerce or in every other aspect of life, people compromise all the time – the pressure of work and other commitments increase and God is relegated to a minor role. As Kierkegaard says:

> ... this press of busyness is like a charm. And it is sad to see how its power swells, how it reaches out seeking always to lay hold on ever-younger victims so that childhood or youth are scarcely allowed the

quiet and the retirement in which the Eternal may unfold a divine growth ... the press of busyness into which one steadily enters further and further, and the noise in which the truth continually slips more and more into oblivion ... It is true that a mirror has the quality of enabling a man to see his image in it, but for this he must stand still.· If he rushes hastily by he sees nothing.' (PH 107–8)

If the individual would really achieve purity of heart and really wishes to relate him or herself wholly to God and to live this relationship out, then 'busyness' and activity can be the biggest temptation. It is so easy to think that what one is doing is 'important' or that it 'matters', but where God is concerned this may be an excuse for the individual to concentrate attention on him or herself and his or her own recognition by the world and not on patient, humble service to God.

Kierkegaard considers that anyone who seriously tries to remain loyal to the eternal and puts the temporal world into second place will *necessarily* suffer. The crowd, the mass of people, will try hard to get such a person to conform to their will, to water down his or her commitment and ensure compromise. If he or she will take this path then popularity and success may well result – but the eternal will have been abandoned. It is worth being clear here that by suffering Kierkegaard does not mean the suffering of illness, disappointment, hurt, etc., to which all human beings are prone. He is referring firstly to the suffering that will necessarily come to anyone who tries to follow Jesus and who puts God in central place. Just as Jesus was despised and rejected by the crowd, so will the same reaction be meted out to any who follow him. Secondly, however, he is referring to the pain of actually trying to become a self, to become what a human being is capable of becoming when this is so different from what human nature will choose if left to its own devices.

Kierkegaard admits some will say that such suffering is 'useless' and does not 'achieve' anything, but this is to look at things from a temporal rather than an eternal perspective. To measure what is worthwhile in terms of results is precisely to objectify religion and to deny its essentially subjective nature. An individual may be alone and abandoned by others because he or she is trying to follow God, but God will never abandon such a one. It is at this point that 'cleverness' comes in; but it is generally a cleverness which convinces the individual that he or she is mistaken, that God does not really want this suffering, that it is better to compromise, to 'achieve' something and to harmonize with the world. This is temptation, albeit a subtle and clever form of temptation.

Kierkegaard's message here is uncompromising and, it must be admitted, out of tune with what many regard as the Christian message. Not many today emphasize suffering, yet for Kierkegaard it is an essential result of discipleship:

> *This is the test: to become and remain a Christian, through sufferings with which no other human sufferings can compare in painfulness and anguish. Yet it is not Christianity that is cruel, nor is it Christ. No, Christ in Himself is gentleness and love ... the cruelty consists in the fact that the Christian has to live in this world and express in the environment of this world what it is to be a Christian ... the more the Christian is inwardly in fear and trembling before God, so much the more is he in dread of every false step, so much the more is he inclined only to accuse himself. In this situation it might sometimes be a comfort to him if others thought well of him. But exactly the opposite is the case ... the more he labours in fear and trembling struggling all the time to be more entirely unselfish, devoted and loving, all the more do men accuse him of self-love ...* (TC 194–5)

Christianity, according to Kierkegaard, requires the individual to live out life focused on God and not on the temporal:

Christianity is still the only explanation of existence which holds water. The earthly existence is suffering; every man has his share, and therefore his dying words are: God be praised, it is done with. This earthly existence is the time of test, is the examination ... You and I are being examined our whole life long. (J 1052)

God chooses and is closest to the despised, the cast-offs of the race, one single, sorry, abandoned wretch, a dreg of humanity. (J 4231)

To love God and to be happy and fortunate in this world are not possible. (J 2443)

The one thing that unites every single man and woman in the world, no matter what their race, their age or the financial circumstance, is their ability to be a single individual relating directly to God. This eliminates all temporal distinctions and makes every human being equal to every other. The only goal in life that can endure through all contingency, through all alterations of circumstances, is the goal of single-mindedly willing to be in relationship with God. If one does this and lives the whole of one's life accordingly, then one will not be afraid of eternity's judgement. All human beings will, after death, have to account for their lives and the accounting will not be in terms of what they have achieved, how much money they have made or how popular they are – no, the accounting will be based on the extent to which they have lived in relationship with God and allowed this relationship to guide every facet of their lives.

In the previous chapter we saw that Kierkegaard insisted that truth is to be found in the individual's subjectivity but that this was not a relativistic claim. The objective truth of Christianity (if, of course, it is true and Kierkegaard accepted this could not be proved) had to be lived out in a day by day relationship to God. Determining whether one is in this relationship is a matter for each individual and, essentially, involves 'willing one thing' and purity of heart. More needs to be said in this area, however, as to how an individual can *discern* whether or not he or she is in a relationship with God – certainly it will necessarily involve love, but Kierkegaard's understanding of Christian love is radical and this will be examined in the next chapter.

9

Works of Love

We have seen that, for Kierkegaard, coming to Christianity involves making a choice between offence at the paradox of the God-Man or faith. Faith requires reason to be set aside and for the individual to depend wholly on God, putting God at the centre of all concerns. However, it would be easy to caricature such a position and to maintain that it is essentially pietistic, requiring only individual faith with no commitment to action in the world – indeed such a charge is frequently levelled at Kierkegaard. However this is to misunderstand him.

Kierkegaard maintains that both faith and works are required for the Christian. The debate between Luther and the Catholic Church is sometimes crudely caricatured as a debate between the primacy of faith and works – but Kierkegaard shows it is not as simple as this:

> ... in every human being there is an inclination either to want to be meritorious when it comes to works or, when faith and grace are to be emphasized, also to want to be free of works as far as possible. Indeed, 'man', this rational creation of God, certainly does not let himself be fooled; he is not a peasant coming to market, he has his eyes open. 'No, it's one or the other,' says man. 'If it is to be works – fine, but then I must also ask for the legitimate yield I have coming from my works, so that they are meritorious. If it is to be grace – fine, but then I must also ask to be free from works – otherwise it surely is not grace. If it is to be works and nevertheless grace, this is indeed foolishness.' Yes,

this is indeed foolishness; that would also be true Lutheranism; that would indeed be Christianity. Christianity's requirement is this: your life should express works as strenuously as possible; then one thing more is required – that you humble yourself and confess: But my being saved is nevertheless grace. The error of the Middle Ages, meritoriousness, was abhorred. But when one scrutinizes the matter more deeply, it is easy to see that people had perhaps an even greater notion that works are meritorious than did the Middle Ages, but they applied grace in such a way that they freed themselves from works. (FSE 16–17)

So works are required but the individual will not see any merit in the works, rather seeing himself being saved only by grace. Similarly in terms of a faith response to God, the individual must venture. He or she must strive to develop a relationship with God but nevertheless hold steadfastly that faith is a free gift from God. Faith depends entirely on God having become man in order to bridge the gap between the human and the Divine. To anyone saying that faith must either be striven for or be a gift, that the two poles cannot be brought together and that there is an either/or here, Kierkegaard would say that it is indeed foolishness – the foolishness that makes Christianity folly to the Greeks and the philosophers.

What, then, does Christianity require from the person who has faith? At one level, Kierkegaard would consider this an inappropriate question. If what was sought was a list of objective criteria against which one could measure whether someone was living a Christian life, then Kierkegaard would maintain that this was to radically misunderstand the issue. As we have seen, faith is essentially subjective and there is no single outer manifestation – not even the virtuous or ethical life since this is not the same as a life lived in relationship with God. The life of faith essentially involves willing one thing – placing God at the centre of everything one does.

However, Kierkegaard is quite specific that a life lived in this way will necessarily involve love. Possibly his most significant book is one that is seldom read and has until recently been out of print for some years in English. This book is entitled *Works of Love* and it was published in 1847. Kierkegaard maintains that most love is preferential and therefore selfish. Love of a partner, of children or of friends is not Christian love – in fact these types of preferential love Kierkegaard considers to be positively dangerous as they tend to encourage an exclusive, inward looking love of a small group which is opposed to the *non-preferential love* which is what Christianity requires. The duty to love one's neighbour is commanded by Christianity – it is a direct consequence of faith. Jesus says *'Thou shalt love ...'* – love is not an optional extra. The command is to love everyone, irrespective of race, colour or creed. It is a command to love irrespective of appearance, irrespective of all temporal or worldly differences. 'Love makes no distinctions – and we must love everyone equally rather than seek to *make* everyone equal' (WL 70).

The task of Christians is not to strive for social equality so that everyone is equal in a worldly sense, but rather to recognize that everyone is equal irrespective of worldly differences. Kierkegaard sees the great equality of all human beings as an equality before God and once this is truly recognized then everyone must be loved equally as children of God. This love is not merely theoretical, it must be a passionate and committed love which is costly and demanding.

Kierkegaard does not reject married love or friendship, still less does he reject the power of the erotic and of sexuality. However he does consider that these loves must not be put into first place – *all* loves, even the love involved in marriage and children, must be secondary to the centrality of the relationship with God. As Kierkegaard says:

Your wife shall first and foremost be your neighbour; the fact that she is your wife is just a narrower definition of your special relationship to her. (WL 141)

In any relationship, God must be the middle term' – each relationship should be a triangle involving two people with God in the middle:

Love cannot be just between people – that would merely be Eros or friendship. Christian love must be between three for God is always the middle term. (WL 46)

As soon as God is eliminated, all loves become selfish. True love of neighbour does not depend on being loved in return – it is unconditional: 'However much the beloved changes, the Lover never varies in his love – Love abides' (WL 281). This applies to God's love of human beings which remains unchanged no matter what we do. *God's love is not earned, it is not a reward for virtue.* God loves human beings as they are and seeks to woo them to be more like Him. Similarly human beings should love unconditionally – which is why forgiveness should come easily to Christians who are really trying to follow Christ as love does not hold grudges and is always ready to think the best of another.

Kierkegaard does not reject self-love – indeed he emphasizes that Jesus called his followers to love others *as themselves*. To really love ourselves we must live in relationship with God and develop to be real individuals. Similarly if we really love others we must seek to bring them to the same position:

The Christian view means this: Truly to love oneself is to love God; truly to love another person is with every sacrifice (even to become hated) to help the other person love God as well. (WL 119)

As John Saxbee pointed out in a paper given at the annual Kierkegaard dinner in the Danish Church in London on the anniversary of Kierkegaard's death on 11 November 1990, Kierkegaard identifies everyone as our neighbour in the global village to which we belong and he re-directs our attention away from the outward and visible 'what' of giving and our loving to the 'how' of Christian love. Saxbee quoted Kierkegaard:

> *If that man famous through eighteen hundred years, the merciful Samaritan, if he had come walking, not riding, on the way from Jericho to Jerusalem where he saw the unfortunate man lying, if he had brought nothing with him whereby he could bind up his wounds, if he had then lifted up the unfortunate man and placed him on his shoulders, carrying him to the nearest inn where the keeper would take in neither him nor the unfortunate one because the Samaritan did not have a penny, if he could only beg and beseech the hard-hearted innkeeper nevertheless to be merciful because it involved a man's life – if therefore he had not ... but no, the tale is not yet done – consequently, if the Samaritan, far from losing patience over this, had gone away carrying the unfortunate man, had sought a softer resting place for the wounded man, had sat by his side, had done everything in his power to halt the loss of blood – but the unfortunate man died in his arms; would he not have been just as merciful, equally as merciful as that merciful Samaritan, or is there some objection to be lodged against calling this the story of the good Samaritan?* (WL 294)

Saxbee says that there is, indeed, no objection to be lodged here and Kierkegaard 'scores a palpable hit'. Everyone can love irrespective of their circumstances just as everyone is to be loved, not because they are inherently lovable but because God commands it. When we pick out some favoured ones to love or when we love those whom we like, then this is not Christian love. Kierkegaard has a parable which draws a parallel with two artists. One artist toured the world looking for someone beautiful to paint and never found anyone adequate to his skill. The other artist stayed at home and found something beautiful to paint in every person he encountered. Which, Kierkegaard asks, is the true artist? Just as with the artists, so it should be with the Christian – we should love others not because they deserve to be loved or because they have lovable features but because all women and men are lovable. If we cannot see this, the fault is in us rather than in the others.

Kierkegaard has a point here which intuitively seems right, but it must be questioned whether all people can be loved in this way. Is it practical to love the SS guard if one is a Jewish prisoner who has just had her baby's brains splattered across a wall? Is it possible for a woman in war-torn Bosnia or Rwanda to love the men who are serially raping her? These challenges are pointed but, if they are valid, they should be directed against Christianity itself and not simply against Kierkegaard. Kierkegaard is surely expressing one of Christ's fundamental commands. Whether this command can be lived in practice is another issue.

(10)

Kierkegaard and the Church

St Augustine spent his life as a Bishop defending the Church from heresies such as that of the Manichees, the Pelagians and the Donatists. For Augustine, salvation lay through membership of the Church — not all those within the Church might be saved but outside the Church there was no salvation. The Roman Catholic Church, even though some of its members were reluctant to deny worthy Protestants a part in the Church of Christ, continued to adopt this position up until the declaration *Lumen Gentium: The Dogmatic Constitution on the Church* in 1965, which deals with the salvation of non-believers. Most great Christian thinkers have, while at times being critical, nevertheless been loyal members of the Church and, if at all, have spoken against it mildly and gently. Kierkegaard was far more ambiguous in his view — in fact he was often downright critical of the Church. For most of his life he attended the Lutheran Church of Denmark regularly and preached at times. He considered ordination at various stages of his life but never took the final step — partly because he felt a call to be a writer and partly because his frustration with the Church was possibly too great. He ended his life with one of the most devastating attacks on the Church ever written. These attacks were made in a series of articles which have been collected together in a book entitled *Attack upon Christendom*. The articles were published between 1854 and 1895.

The occasion for the attack was the funeral oration following the death of Bishop Mynster. Kierkegaard had known the old

Bishop well for much of his life and when Professor Martensen delivered an address calling Mynster a 'witness for the truth', Kierkegaard's patience snapped. For Kierkegaard, a 'witness to the truth' was a quite specific term – it ranked with the apostles as the highest of Christian categories. Mynster's virtue, in Kierkegaard's eyes, was that he had fully recognized that he did not belong in this category at all. Kierkegaard saw Martensen's funeral oration as a cynical exercise in drawing attention to the orator, namely Martensen himself, who sought the bishopric made vacant by Mynster's death. Kierkegaard withheld his attack until Martensen was appointed and then let forth his protest.

The protest started with an attack on Martensen but it soon widened to an attack on the whole Church, on priests and on the social institution which the Church had become. Kierkegaard considered that many priests and churches no longer proclaimed the Christian gospel, instead they proclaimed a message of comfort and good cheer. They sought a comfortable 'living' for themselves and the Church provided them with security, respectability and a position in society. Kierkegaard did not think that Christianity was comfortable. Priests and churches were 'making a fool out of God' by proclaiming something that was utterly alien to the Christianity of the New Testament.

Some commentators have said that Kierkegaard's criticism of the Church was a late development, but this is not the case. His negative views on the clergy and 'Christendom' (which identified the Church with the nation) were present throughout his writings. One of his books, *Judge for Yourself*, asks his reader to visit any church on a Sunday and to judge for themselves whether what is there proclaimed is the same as the Christianity of the New Testament which involved passion, commitment and total dedication:

'Christendom' is not the Church of Christ ... Not by any means. No, I say that 'Christendom' is twaddle which has clung to Christianity like a cobweb to a fruit, and now is so polite as to want to be mistaken for Christianity ... The sort of existence which the millions of 'Christendom' give evidence of has absolutely no relation to the New Testament' (AC 192)

Kierkegaard is, therefore, not rejecting the true Church of Christ made up of the fellowship of those who are sincerely and with passion trying to follow Christ in humble obedience – what he is rejecting is the institutional Church which is a travesty of the real thing.

The same point is applied to the New Testament which Kierkegaard sees as being 'sanitized' and diluted by the Church. As one of his parables says:

The New Testament ... regarded as a guide for Christians [can] ... become pretty much like a guidebook to a particular country when everything in that country has been totally changed. Such a guidebooks serves no longer the serious purpose of being useful to travellers in that country, but at the most it is worth reading for amusement. When one is making the journey easily by railways, one reads in the guidebook 'Here is Woolf's Gullet where one plunges 70,000 fathoms down under the earth', while one sits and smokes one's cigar in the snug cafe, one reads in the guidebook 'here a band of robbers has its stronghold from which it issues to assault the travellers and maltreat them', here it is, etc. Here it is; that is, here it was; for now (it is very amusing to imagine how it was), now there is no Woolf's Gullet but the railway, and no robber band but a snug cafe. (AC 111)

Kierkegaard does not reject 'the guidebook', which is the New Testament, indeed he is affirming its continuing relevance and importance to life today. What it is to be a human being and the journey each person has to make are essentially the same as when the New Testament was written – but so often this is not recognized and the Bible becomes a historical curiosity. Kierkegaard rejects those who dismiss the relevance of the Bible as well as the safety and security of those in the train (the Church) who no longer feel themselves individually accountable to it. We can see here the influence of the Reformation idea of an 'open Bible', giving all believers direct access to the word of God. For Kierkegaard, although he was aware of current developments in biblical scholarship, the Bible nevertheless represented a clear handbook which could guide someone who wished to live a life accountable to God. Kierkegaard also criticized those biblical scholars who spend their time in critical examination of the Bible rather than being radically accountable to it. He asks his reader to imagine a king who issued a royal command to the whole population of a country but instead of the royal command being obeyed and listened to, it becomes the object of analysis and huge amounts of literature written about its style and origins. Instead of 'true seriousness' representing radical accountability to the Bible, biblical scholars transform seriousness into textual exegesis (FSE 58–9).

Dean Bloch, in an article in April 1855, threatened Kierkegaard with 'ecclesiastical sanction' because of his attacks. Kierkegaard's response was characteristic:

> *If I do not reform, the Dean would have me punished ecclesiastically. And how? Indeed the punishment is cruelly devised; it is so cruel that I counsel the women to have their smelling salts at hand in order not to faint when they hear it. If I do not reform, the church door will be closed to me. Horrible! So then, if I do not reform, I shall be shut out, excluded from hearing on Sundays during the quiet hours, the eloquence of the witnesses to the truth.* (AC 47)

Kierkegaard's sarcasm is obvious – the Bible is still available to him and he is still accountable to and loved by God. The 'true worship of God consists quite simply in doing God's will' and the Church is not absolutely necessary for this (AC 219). Soon Kierkegaard came to feel that he could not in conscience continue to 'make a fool of God' by taking part in Sunday worship. Salvation does not depend on the dictates of priests – but upon God. The priests make a good living and acquire respect and admiration by talking in lofty terms on Sundays, but what they talk about is intended to bring comfort to their flock and security to themselves – they do not talk about Christ's message.

In a parable, Kierkegaard likened the Church to a building into which farmyard geese went each Sunday. An elder goose preached and talked about the love of the great Goose in the sky and how he had made geese with wings so that they could fly. Every time the great Goose's name was mentioned all the geese bowed – and so it went on every Sunday. They came and went into the building but their life was otherwise the same. One goose, however, was foolish enough to take the story seriously and instead of being concerned with life in the farmyard spent his time trying to fly and to use the wings he had been given. Everyone said how foolish he was, yet finally he took to the air, flew around and came back and told everyone that the stories were true and that the other geese, also, could use their wings – but they ignored him. And so life went on, until Christmas when all the geese were cooked for Christmas dinner except for the one who had learned to use his wings.

Kierkegaard rejected much that was comfortable and normally accepted. As we have seen, he thought that marriage brought real dangers of a loss of individuality; that ceremonies such as baptism and confirmation were mere outward symbols while what Christianity sought was an inner, subjective transformation. He thought that the task of Christians must be to love others as they love themselves by helping to draw others to making a decision to become involved with God, and that membership of a Church was not sufficient to make someone a Christian. He considered the incarnation to be a paradox, an offence to reason, and that anyone becoming involved with Christ would inevitably suffer as a result.

One of Denmark's greatest social reformers, Grundtvig, lived at the same time as Kierkegaard. Grundtvig had an enormous influence on Danish education and Danish social policy – in almost every town in Denmark a Grundtvig high school is to be found. Kierkegaard, however, said that 'Grundtvig can never properly be said to have fought for Christianity; he really only fought for something earthly' (AC 185). The community and social policy were not Kierkegaard's concern and he would have thought that the concern of the Church with these matters today had tended to minimize the importance of the individual and the individual's accountability to God. Social change would come not from a transformation of society but from a transformation of individuals – and becoming an individual is the most difficult task of all, which Church membership can sometimes prevent as social convention within the Church is substituted for passion and real Christian commitment.

Kierkegaard certainly did not argue for the abolition of the Church of Christ – far from it. What he warned against was the danger of mistaking the institution of the Church for Christ's Church. He saw his task as being to 'reintroduce Christianity in Christendom'. He thought it would be easier in a missionary situation to bring Christianity to people who had never heard of it than to bring people to see what Christianity involved – when they already thought that they were Christians. This was his difficulty – and his entire authorship involves trying to get people to sit up and take notice. He expected his books to be largely ignored or to be pored over by academics – but his task was to seek 'his reader' who would read quietly and would allow the whole of life to be changed by accepting the challenge that Christianity really represents – or else rejecting it. Better, he would say, to be offended and to reject Christianity than to take part in the travesty of

Christianity which the Church has so often become.

In the final months of his life, Kierkegaard used to deliberately sit outside the Church on Sunday instead of joining in the worship – although he insisted on continuing to pay tithes of his income to the Church just in case anyone thought he would derive financial advantage from not attending.

He died less than six months later having collapsed in the street. He died giving thanks to God for having educated him on what it was to be a Christian. Throughout his life, he saw God's hand guiding him – although this guidance was seen in retrospect and not at the time. He looked forward to heaven, where he would have nothing else to do but to give thanks.

Since his death, Kierkegaard has had a huge influence on many seminal figures including Ibsen, Karl Barth, Kafka, W. H. Auden, C. S. Lewis, Gabriel Marcel, R. S. Thomas and many others – however there is no space here to discuss these influences.

The fact that this book, therefore, has not considered Kierkegaard's motivations and his psychological state is a deliberate policy. If Kierkegaard's authorship succeeds in its aim then such analysis is beside the point – perhaps he may be held to have succeeded despite the obstacles in his path, perhaps he succeeded because of these obstacles. The important point is whether he succeeds or not, not why he succeeds or fails. If he fails in his objectives, then analysis of his background may provide reasons to explain or excuse his failure and these may be interesting, but it is only an analysis of failure.

This book has not set out to explain whether Kierkegaard's enterprise fails or succeeds – rather it is concerned to make clear what his enterprise was and so that you, the reader, can be motivated to read further and then decide for yourself whether or not he succeeds. Such an approach is entirely faithful to Kierkegaard's own intention.

Suggested Further Reading

Kierkegaard's Own Works

This book cannot do justice to Kierkegaard's thought and there is no substitute for reading his works for yourself – although they are not always easy. It is better to read Kierkegaard in the original than any number of commentators. The most accessible of his books include the following:

Works of Love (On the nature of Christian love)
Concluding Unscientific Postscript (Central themes include truth as subjectivity and indirect communication)
Purity of Heart is to will one thing (Kierkegaard's great spiritual classic)
Fear and Trembling (Discussion of Abraham and Isaac)
Philosophical Fragments (Comparison of Jesus and Socrates)
Attack upon Christendom (Collection of essays critical of the Church)
Either/Or (Long and not easy to get into. Contrasts the aesthetic and ethical stages)
Sickness unto Death (Analyses despair and the development of the self)
Stages on Life's Way
Eighteen Edifying Discourses (Specifically religious themes)
The Present Age (Kierkegaard's views on democracy and government)

There have been many editions of Kierkegaard's works. An international translation team under Howard and Edna Hong have been issuing, through Princeton University Press, new editions of most of his works and these are in-print and available. The notes at the back of these editions are comprehensive and, for academic use, very helpful. Previous editions are, however, just as good if they can be obtained second-hand. *Either/Or, Sickness unto Death* and *Fear and Trembling* are available in Penguin Classics.

Recommended Critical Works

Evans, C. S., *Kierkegaard's Fragments and Postscript*, Humanities Press, 1983.

Kimmse, B. H., *Kierkegaard in Golden Age Denmark*, Indiana University Press, 1990.

Malantschuk, Gregor, *Kierkegaard's Way to the Truth*, Reitzel, Copenhagen.

McCracken, D., *The Scandal of the Gospels*, Oxford University Press, 1994.

Oden, T. C., ed., *Parables of Kierkegaard*, Princeton University Press, 1989.

Acknowledgements

My thanks are due to many who have influenced me in more than twenty years of reading Kierkegaard. Books and articles written by scholars have, of course, been a significant influence and particular mention must be made of those by C. Stephen Evans, Walter Lowrie, Gregor Malantschuk, Douglas Steere, David Swenson, Neils Thulstrup and Julia Watkin. In addition, many former students and friends at my College of the University of London and others have helped with different insights and in discussions – there have been many of these but I would particularly include Anne Baker, Jude Bullock, Helen Costigane, Catherine Cowley, William Devine, Ivana Dolejsova, Rob Hampson, John Handford, Michael McClure, Felicity McCutcheon, Terri Murray, Paul O'Reilly, Anne-Marie Quigg, Paul Rout, Ann-Marie Ryan, Stewart Sutherland, Elijah Timmerman, Peter Tyler, Rodney Ward, John Waters and my wife Anne. My thanks are also due to Pastor and Mrs Fabricius and the community of the Danish Church in London who every year go to a great deal of trouble to host an annual Kierkegaard dinner on the anniversary of his death – the day which, for Kierkegaard, any Christian should regard as their 'birth-day'. If anyone is ever interested in attending this event, please let me know.

PETER VARDY

Heythrop College, University of London, London W8 5HQ.

Index